IF YOU REALLY LOVED ME

Emma Cantons

Andrews UK Limited

First published worldwide by
Andrews UK Limited
The Hat Factory
Bute Street
Luton
LU1 2EY

www.andrewsuk.com

Contents

Acknowledgements

It goes without saying that my main thanks are to Victoria and my children, and after that to our mums, Mary and Maria-Jesus; My twin sister, Sarah (Queen of the World); Mike; Holly; Lucy and her family, all of whom have shown us such love and provided so much tea.

I would like especially to thank Caroline Grayson for being an oasis of reason when I'd all but lost mine, and for creating such a beautiful and moving vow renewal for us; Sharon Fillingham for more wisdom than any individual has a right to; Cathy Galvin for her enduring friendship but more especially for reading first draughts and encouraging me to keep going; Helen Shreeve for her invaluable help in getting this book ready for publication, to say nothing of her kindness and understanding; All the myriad Angels on the transgender support website, UK Angels, who shared so honestly, listened so patiently and sent me so much virtual chocolate to keep me going. Sue and Becca; Amy; Mercia and Mary; Paula and Sophie; Mel; Imelda and Richard; Carolyn and Marek; Becky; LiD.; Pandora and Robert; Steve; Garry and Catherine; Steve and Heidi and everyone at TDCom.

I would like to thank Helen Shreeve and Lisa Jenkinson for arranging for us to be on Saturday Live on Radio 4; Richard Coles and Sian Williams for enabling us to tell our story and asking all the right questions; AUK publishers for offering to publish this book and sorting out all the technical stuff.

Finally I would like to thank everyone who felt challenged by us but kept trying and made their own transitional journey of understanding.

For the Duck, the Kitten and the Goth

Chapter One

This is the story of how I married a man who turned out to be a woman but still lived happily ever after. It isn't a story I expected to be telling, and sometimes I look around me and wonder at the strange normality of it all. Sometimes I look around me and wonder what the hell just happened. I didn't always believe that it would turn out how it has, but I hoped. This is the story of how I found out what was possible, if two people really loved each other. This is a love story.

I was born in 1962 in London, one of twin girls with an older brother of nearly two. In 1964 we were joined by my younger sister. My parents were creative and intelligent, but their lives had been blighted by an illness that hit my father a year after they married. Brain injured, paralysed and epileptic he was not an easy man to live with. That last sentence was a massive understatement, but you get the idea I"m sure.

We children were all born after the cataclysm of Dad's illness. I wandered off to teacher training college at 18, because some teacher told me I should and I couldn't think of a good answer. I met my first husband as he was in his final year at Cambridge. He was everything my father wasn't, quiet and logical, so I decided this was love and stuck to him like a limpet. Not one of my best decisions. I think he married me because I, or maybe his parents, told him to, and he couldn't think of a good answer. It was not a happy marriage, but two beautiful children came out of it, my son in 1989 and my daughter in 1993, so it wasn't a complete waste of time. In 1999 everything that could happen, happened. My older brother died when his motorcycle collided with a car on the M40, Rob, then 10, was finally diagnosed as autistic and my marriage ended, to rousing cries of "About time too" from all who loved me. 1999 was not a good year, I call it 'the year of vodka'. Turns out

1

vodka doesn't resolve anything, and there was a day when I was on my way to my daughter Ellie's school, that I considered driving into a lamp-post, thus, in my mind, simplifying everything. A split second later it occurred to me that if I felt that miserable it really was time to change things. So I did.

It was scary moving out of the family home with no certain future. The flat the children and I went into was in a bit of a state. The previous owners had sealed up every source of outside air in an attempt to keep warm. It hadn't worked, except the sealing up part, which was triumphant. The place was damp and rotting. I guess that's why I could afford it. Luckily for me by simply opening the windows and removing the wallpaper from the air bricks (bless their determination), all signs of damp miraculously disappeared and I was left with a rather sweet home. I battled with the local authority to get funding for my son's education. That meant residential placements - schools specially focused on children like him. They were not in London. The one I found was just outside Southampton, an hour and a half's drive away. Expensive stuff and not the sort of thing any council can afford to hand out without being sure it's the right thing. Still, it is painful that in order to get help for your child, you must constantly admit what they can't do, why they are not normal and what a nightmare each day is. It goes against the grain. Like all mothers my default setting is boasting and pride. I thought when he was diagnosed, that I would be given a helpful pamphlet, 'How to raise your autistic child' and a list of useful phone numbers and addresses of schools. Ha Ha. For anyone else with a disabled child reading this, all together now - Ha.

Eventually though, everyone involved bit the bullet and I sewed labels into his socks and shirts and trousers. Of all the hurts involved in arriving on this planet with a disability, like a spaceman in a faulty spacesuit, it was his having to live with labels in his socks that made me cry. I took him to the residential school. I had been warned that long drawn out goodbyes did not help the difficulty of the situation, and I was to bring him to the house group, say a brisk goodbye and go. You have to understand that up to this point I had been my son's liaison with the world. His speech was hard to understand and he was very nervous of strangers, new situations and change. I knew all the things he couldn't handle, and how to handle them. Going to a residential school was a huge step for him. As I hugged him goodbye and told him it would be fine he whispered in my ear, "I can't do this". Every maternal instinct screamed, get him out of here, don't abandon him, save him. But I knew if I really wanted to save him, from a life that only functioned through me, this was the only way. I left. It is the hardest thing I have ever done. Ever.

I still believe, however that it was the right thing. Life began to find an equilibrium. During term time, while he was away, I could work. I started a business called 'The Piano Lady'. I taught in schools, I ran choirs, I ran toddler music groups and worked with disabled children, including two groups of autistic children. On the last day of each term I would drive down to Southampton and collect him. The holidays,were a full time occupation, with no tea-breaks, very little sleep and definitely no going out. On the last day of the holidays, I would drive him back to Southampton, get home at about ten at night and then back to work the next day. It was rather unremitting, but I was able to support myself and my children. We bought furniture and plants for the garden. I felt pretty damn proud of myself.

I had been single for about three years and was, I liked to think, a self-sufficient free standing adult. I kept all my bills in a small wicker box called the picnic basket of destiny. When I felt brave enough I would open it and deal with the grown up things inside, like insurance documents, bank statements and special needs assessments.

It made me very happy that my kids were safe, my bills were paid and I was no longer married. I got to be me all the time. I can remember the power of that realisation. I think I had spent a lot of time trying to be what others expected of me, and I did it so successfully that I got lost somewhere. What I wanted, what might make me happy, these things were not only a mystery to me, I wasn't even thinking about them. On the first night I moved into the maisonette with my children I sat on the damp and smelly shag pile carpet, I had no furniture at that point. I had tacked a sheet over the window and I had very little money in the bank. It was wonderful. No matter how difficult things were it would be me dealing with them, as me. When I had time to think of it, I was lonely, but mostly I was way to busy to think of it.

Then, one evening, a friend came round with a bottle of wine to watch a movie, her husband, she said, would join us later. When my son was at home this was my version of going out. We quickly got into a discussion about how lonely I must be. I explained that I was self-sufficient, free-standing, and had a picnic basket of destiny. I had no need of a man, and unless one was going to turn up in my living room, I had precious little chance of meeting one.

The doorbell rang, on cue, as I finished this hymn to feminine independence. It was her husband, and he'd brought a friend. I had actually met this friend a couple of times before. Once at their house, when we had all set the world to rights over tea and biscuits, and once when he turned up with her at a Salsa club. His father was French and his mother Spanish - it was a good mix. His name was Anthony and he was lovely, but he had never called so I assumed that was that.

Salsa dancing, I should mention, had been the once a week night out with my sister and a friend that kept me going. It was where I remembered what fun was, and how much I missed it. Like a long fused bomb it ticked away inside my marriage, not belonging to my married life but standing in direct contrast, highlighting everything that was wrong and missing. Fun, I eventually decided, should not be an optional extra. I think I also reached that conclusion about love. When I had to explain to my children that mummy and daddy were not going to be together anymore, I told them this: "There are some things you want, like chocolate and bicycles, and if you can't have them, you'll still be o.k. There are other things that you need, and you can't choose to live without them, like air and water and love." Not an optional extra.

Anyway, back to the movie night. There I stood letting them in at the front door. Friend's husband came in first saying, "I've brought Anthony, I hope you don't mind." Then Anthony walked in. Well no, he stood in the doorway and I stood there and the universe shifted. It just did. It was as though he'd come home. We completely recognised each other. Technically it wasn't love at first sight, because I had already seen him on two separate occasions, but it was sudden and instant, so in my mind it qualifies. I know this sounds overly romantic. I am willing to admit that no orchestras played, and local wildlife remained stoically un-melodic. Nonetheless, we both experienced something very profound and after it everything was different.

He never left. We took up our life together as if it were the most natural thing in the world. To wait any longer would have been ridiculous. At the end of the working day he came home - our home. Two weeks later he proposed. I've no idea what took him so long. I had never been proposed to before. I had been involved in negotiations of 'isn't it time you asked me to marry you' which is not the same. This was the fantasy. Completely surprised but utterly sure. Lovely. Suddenly my life went from I am woman I am strong, to fairy tale. Instead of kindly pitying the hard slog of my life, people expressed wonder at my luck. I was engaged to a gorgeous fun and kind man who was seven years my junior. Classic tall dark and handsome.

Ellie seemed to find a bond with him immediately. He talked to her in a way that said he respected what she had to say. What she thought mattered. It wasn't an act to 'win her round' it was sincere and I think she sensed it. He was endlessly willing to help with homework and play sock football with her. We went on a day trip to Legoland. I knew we were getting a bit carried away with the sweets and souvenirs, but I hadn't been able to give my kids any of these things and suddenly it was all possible. It also meant I could look after my son while Anthony prevented Ellie from being left out. A lot of her childhood had been dictated to by her brother's needs. If he couldn't handle it, she couldn't do it. Parks, swings, swimming pools, crowds. She missed out on a lot. Even more amazingly, my son began to form a trust with Anthony that meant sometimes, I could focus on Ellie. Anthony took his role as step-father to an autistic child very seriously. He came to all the meetings, found out as much as he could about autism and would jump down the throat of anyone who suggested that all that was needed was a firm hand to make all the problems disappear. I think my boy very quickly sensed that this was someone who was going to be there for him, to fight his corner and listen to what he had to say.

Anthony also had an encyclopedic knowledge of graphic novels (which I imagined were comics, but apparently not) and rock music. This proved a real winner, because my son was fascinated by these things, and I hadn't the first idea. I like jazz. Ella Fitzgerald and Louis Armstrong. Who the bass guitarist is in Iron Maiden? Sorry, not the faintest idea. Unlike me, Anthony could engage in conversations about best albums and gigs for hours at a time. Or the 'Sandman' series. Don't ask. I'm told it's very good.

He was learning how to be a parent at speed. Of course every now and then he'd make some rookie error. For instance, when passing under a low bridge at Legoland with a nine year old girl on your shoulders - duck. She got a bump on her head, nothing worse, but poor Anthony was mortified. She, once she'd got over the surprise of being walked into a bridge, thought it was hilarious, particularly Anthony's horror at his own stupidity. He promised not to spoil her, but he couldn't help himself. If he saw something cool and interesting that he thought she'd like, he just had to get it. Having spent a good few years wondering if there were enough coins down the back of the sofa to buy half a dozen eggs, I was happy to go along with his generosity. Suddenly life was just better.

One of the things that was a lot better was sex. To be fair it didn't have much to live up to so far, but even so there was an instant freedom between us, a sureness that either of us could express themselves without fear and would find acceptance. Anthony told me very early on that he got a big turn on from wearing women's underwear. Not anything I'd experienced before, but it worked for us and was happily embraced. Passionate, spontaneous and loving, why had I ever settled for less than this? He had a name for this feminine part of himself. It didn't suit him, or indeed her, I told him I would call her Vicky. Victoria is my middle name and as we were two halves of the same soul, it seemed right.

Anthony was also infertile, it had been a great source of sadness to him initially. In his mid twenties he had gone to the doctor to assess his fertility after a relationship he had been in for several years ended. He had begun to question why there had never been so much as a false alarm over the years. The discovery that his sperm were all dead or deformed must have come as a shock to such a young man, but he saw no alternative but to accept his situation. He had come to terms with it long before we met. Though it may sound selfish, Anthony's infertility was a bonus to me, freeing me as it did from the worry of accidentally becoming pregnant.

At first my family were anxious that this was all too sudden and they were relieved that we intended to wait two years before actually marrying. We had all been through a great deal as a family, and we were very protective of each other. My father had eventually had to be sectioned to the Maudsley in South London, when the medication designed to control his epilepsy began to make him quite quite mad. We all had to go elsewhere, immediately.

I remember walking away from the house with a carrier bag containing a nighty and a toothbrush. I was 19 and not entirely ready for the adult world. The housing association then decided we weren't 'making use' of the family home and took it away dumping anything we couldn't organize to remove within a week into a skip. Leaving home is not something any of us got to do, it sort of left us. It didn't make for very stable choices in our twenties, (see page 1: earlier decision to marry wrong person), though it did make us all excellent at de-cluttering. More importantly it made us a very tight knit and protective family. We looked out for each other.

The two years came and went and we were still blissfully happy, devoted to each other and to both children. All the hardness went out of life. If I had to face something challenging - usually more funding battles for special needs provision, Anthony was there. Calm, loving and helpful. I found myself having doors opened for me, shopping carried. Every day began and ended with 'I love you'. Vicky was always there, but always private. We had a lot of fun, all the time. This, I decided, was how life was meant to be.

Looking back on those early days, I was already concerned about how dominant the feminine part of Anthony's personality might prove to be, but I believed it to be an aspect of who he was, a private bedroom aspect, not all of him. He was certainly kinder than any man I had ever known. There was a side of him that seemed in touch with a gentler nurturing gender, but he was also a determined provider and protector. My anxieties about this other person, this female identity that lurked in the secret background of our life, finally found words. I was determined that it couldn't ever be allowed to take over our family.

One day not long after the proposal I ended up asking Anthony for a guarantee that Vicky would never 'come out of the bedroom' because I needed a husband and my children needed a dad. Anthony said 'of course I understand'. I was hugely relieved and we left it at that. In retrospect, with the glorious advantage of hindsight and a much much greater understanding of the transgender experience, that was an impossible promise for Anthony to make, and an impossible promise for him to refuse to make. He promised it, I believe, because he desperately wanted to be able to live this life with no more complications to be faced. No coming out, no rejection and no surgery. He would suppress his feminine self and all would be well.

Logically it was the easiest path to take. Anthony didn't want to find himself somewhere in the middle of the gender spectrum, he, like the rest of us, expected to be just a boy or just a girl. The feeling that he was a girl had been contradicted by everyone around him ever since he could express the idea and he had tried to conform to that. Everyone around him confirmed he was he. When he looked in the mirror, there was a he. He had fallen in love with me and we were the happiest of families. Surely that must mean he was a perfectly normal heterosexual man. Why couldn't this be the truth? And yet and yet.

I was blissfully unaware of all these inner torments. For me, he was clearly a man and he loved me. I was happy. My sister had been worried that I must have presented the less nutty version of myself, until she met Anthony and saw we were both as quirky as each other. Everyone could see how happy we were, how secure the children felt and how right this was. We were a golden couple, ideally matched. An infertile man who had finally found himself with a ready made family against all expectation, and a single mother who had suddenly found love and care when she really had given up on the idea. How lucky were we? Smugness may not be a very noble sentiment, but I allowed myself odd moments of thinking, 'well, this IS going better than expected'.

We were married on the 18th of June 2005 at the Church of the English Martyrs in Streatham. We had - good Lord - seven bridesmaids and my twin sister as matron of honour. Trumpets and flowers, Salsa bands and dinner for a lot of people. It was all very wonderful and we had had a great deal of fun planning it. Ellie even wore a miniature version of my dress. All our friends came and all my family, except my son, because a wedding is the gathering together of all the things that would have phased him at that time - crowds, noise and and me not focussing my attention exclusively on him. Although Anthony's father had died in 2002 and most of his family lived in Canada and couldn't come, his mother and her cousin were there and the church was full.

The party that followed was everything we hoped for. It was a beautiful day. Our first dance was to a classic spanish love song, 'Besame' it means 'kiss me'.

> Besame, besame mucho
> Como si fuera esta la noche
> La ultima vez
>
> Besame, besame mucho
> Que tengo miedo a perderte
> Perderte despues
>
> Kiss me, Kiss me so much
> As though tonight might be
> The last time
>
> Kiss me kiss me so much
> Because I'm afraid of loosing you
> Afterwards.

Everything was perfect. We both felt rescued from half lives. Where before relationships had been fraught and stressful, ours was relaxed and happy. I had no thought in my head of how meaningful the words of that song would become to me as our lives unfolded.

It lasted for about four years before something began to change. It was a subtle something, and it had nothing to do with how much we loved each other. That, through everything, has never been an issue. How we felt about each other on that first night, standing in the doorway and knowing that everything had changed, that is the truth of our love. Honestly, undying love can be a bit of a nuisance at times. Something else had changed. Anthony seemed to be carrying a heavier and heavier burden. Where once he had been relaxed and endlessly playful, now he seemed sadder and more stressed by daily life. Everything challenged him. He just stopped smiling. I couldn't work out what had gone wrong, as far as I could see we were on exactly the same path we had started out on. Nothing had changed and yet everything was different. He was obviously dealing with something terribly painful. I needed to understand and I wanted to help, but most of all I wanted to make it go away.

We talked about his childhood and about his relationship with his father. We talked especially about his transvestite behaviour. He told me how he had gone out, years ago, in a dress to a tea shop and met a female friend. He told me how girlfriends in the past had rejected him when he had told them about his desire to dress as a female. He also began to talk about his belief that this was more than just a part of Anthony. This Vicky, this was who he really was. Anthony wanted to talk more and more about this 'feminine' part of his personality and his desire to express it. I remember saying to him that as far as I could understand it, he had a male body but a female brain. Something must have happened while he was developing in the womb, but the bottom line was, he had come out male. Very sad and everything, bad luck and all that, but there was no acceptable solution, or at least one that I felt ready to even contemplate. It was the often used description of transexuals as the 'woman trapped in a man's body'. Best place for her, I thought.

Although I was on the surface calmly discussing these things with him, in my head panic was rising. The news that he had once sat in a tea shop in a dress, shocked me. This was meant to be a sexual game, how had it expressed itself by sitting in a shop chatting about the weather and drinking tea? What was being described didn't fit the explanation I had in my head. What was being described was going to change my world and I didn't want my world to change, it had already changed once and it was perfect, it didn't need further alterations. I convinced myself that everything would be fine as long as I could 'control' this part of him. Though between the two of us, I felt at ease with the feminine version of Anthony, it was, as far as I was concerned, still Anthony. What ever games we played he was a man so that meant I was a straight woman. Nothing to frighten the horses. I was adamant this was a private pleasure not for anyone else's consumption, certainly not in front of the children. I told him we needed him to be him, that this female aspect was just going to have to keep itself under wraps. He had married me and become the children's' step-dad, that was the deal and that's what he must do. He agreed.

He agreed to something that he had no more power to control than I did, but I don't think he really understood that any more than I did. These were the foundations of a great deal of unhappiness that we were going to have to deconstruct before we could make our way forward. I wish I had known then the absolute futility of trying to make someone be something they're not, but I didn't. That particular life lesson was just beginning.

There is a parallel here with my son's diagnosis of autism. I knew, from a very early age, maybe a year, maybe less, that there was something different about my lovely boy. I worried and fretted about his development, his inability to hold his head up, or sit upright without tumbling over. His incredible sleeplessness, and his distress, his violent screaming distress, at all sorts of things, especially unexpected things, and choice. Health visitors and doctors reassured me he was 'going through a phase' and that he would 'grow out of it'. In my heart of hearts I knew that whatever this was it was a permanent part of my lad and no amount of growing would take him magically out of it. But I so wanted to believe they were right. I ignored those nagging doubts and trusted it would get better. It got worse, of course, why wouldn't it? He's autistic, it's not nits. There is no shampoo for this one. In retrospect I wish I had known earlier, had got him the right help earlier, maybe it would have spared him some of the awful suicidal depression he went through, and maybe not.

The parallel then, is that, deep down, I knew that what Anthony was telling me about himself, was not some temporary delusion and I was not, no matter how much he loved me, going to be able to make him not be this. That knowledge though, was deep deep down. It was a knot in the stomach, an unspoken, un-worded fear. Back in the main world, I wasn't having it and I kidded myself I had been firm but fair. Vicky would stay under wraps. Problem solved.

To watch someone you love slip away from you is of course, heartbreaking, but not being able to talk to anyone about it is worse. I felt so miserable. I couldn't see any way forward and yet I was too ashamed to talk to anyone. I didn't want anyone to know that my beautiful handsome husband thought he was part female and fantasized about having breasts. I didn't want to know it. If I'm being really really honest, and there seems little point in writing this if I'm not going to be honest, I didn't find the idea of my lover having breasts repellent, it was just the idea of anybody else knowing that that was what was going on. What others would know about our relationship and our sex life and how they might judge it, seemed extremely important to me. I know that was hypocritical but the part of it that was worst in my mind, was the invasion of my privacy.

For some people privacy is a minor issue and for others it is a medium issue. For me it has always been THE issue. I'm not sure when I got so protective of my every thought. I could not have written this book five years ago, because I simply wouldn't have been willing to share any of it. Not a word. Like a cast iron body suit, privacy, not sharing my feelings, my true feelings at any rate, had always been my survival mechanism. I was the worst, and the best person, to find myself in a situation that blew my absolute need for privacy out of the water. It was good for me and it needed to happen but it hurt. I clung to my privacy like a drowning man to a cast iron body suit, with nearly the same result.

So I didn't share this huge fear. The awful knowledge that my whole life with Anthony was going to turn out to be a sham, that I was heading for another failed marriage and no one was going to know about it until it was too late. There wasn't going to be any helpful advice. Who knew about this stuff? I invested a great deal of energy worrying about how stupid everyone would think I was for being so happy when the whole thing turned out to be a mistake. Surely, they would say, you must have known? How could you marry someone without understanding something so profoundly central to them? I didn't envisage any compassion, only derision. My friends would be sad to know how little I expected of them. It is, of course, always about the self and the derision was self inflicted, nobody else was laughing. How could they? Nobody else knew.

Anthony and I had a conversation just before Christmas of 2008 in which it all came to a head. Anthony wanted to talk about Vicky, about the pleasure it gave him. It made me anxious because this 'alternative' person, as I saw her, seemed to be taking over every spare moment. I asked him the question I didn't really want to know the answer to. Would he, actually, be happier as Vicky, as a woman? Did he not want to be my husband or my kids step-dad? These two things, I made it very clear to him, were mutually exclusive. Choose. He couldn't answer. I was devastated, I wept, I shouted, I demanded, but I couldn't bear what that silence meant. I knew something was happening that I wouldn't be able to stop. It felt as though I was standing on the smooth snowy surface of an avalanche about to break free. Why would I think I could stop an avalanche? Understanding that it couldn't be stopped took me a long time.

We got through Christmas without mentioning that conversation once. It was as though the thing I had asked for had happened. That unanswered question had never been. This was the perfect scenario, the way I had wanted it. everything as it had promised to be on our wedding day. But where before I had relaxed confidently into my reality, now I felt like it was the last dance on the Titanic. This wonderful happy perfect relationship had hit an iceberg and no one but us knew there was a problem. The question was not would it sink, the question was, had we got any lifeboats and would we all fit? We just stopped talking about it and I hoped it would go away.

Then, one night in January of 2009, lying in bed together, his arms wrapped tight around me as he always did, Anthony said "I can't do this anymore". I knew exactly what he meant but I desperately didn't want to. I asked him "What?", daring him to say the unsayable, but he said it anyway. "I can't be Anthony, it's not who I am. I'm a woman, this isn't my right body. I look in the mirror and I see this male face and this male body and it's not me".

The shock froze me. The fear locked down. I calmly told Anthony that we needed to deal with this mental health problem. These thoughts were irrational, he was a man. "Look in the mirror for God's sake. I understand you want to be a woman, but you're not. If you make yourself look like a woman, I will leave. That will be the end. If you really love me, you won't do this. If you really love me you won't be this. End of discussion". Certainly not the response Anthony needed but it was my trump card, my last ditch attempt to make this not be. Was I willing to blackmail him into living the rest of his life 'wrong' on the inside as long as it worked for me? Was this what it would mean to really love me? At that moment I was not thinking of Anthony's needs at all. I was thinking of what I wanted to be the truth and what would be the simplest truth for my children. I was angry, so very angry, that he had even mentioned the possibility of exposing my children to anything other than unending happiness. I wasn't thinking at all really, I was terrified.

The next morning we did all the normal things. We made breakfast, fed the cat and got Ellie into school as though everything was normal. As soon as we were alone though, the discussion started again. Anthony spoke of his need to express his true self, his feminine self. I was adamant that could not be allowed to happen. Maybe when Ellie had left home, got through university, maybe I might allow it, but not now. We talked about how long he had felt like this. That was a shock. It turned out his first experiences had been as a very small child, not understanding why he couldn't dress like the other girls, or why he had to go into the boy's line at infants school. He had secretly dressed all his life. As a tiny child he had put on his grandmother's nighty and curled up next to her in bed. I don't know if she found that alarming or sweet. I found it alarming. Again I was confronted with the idea that this was nothing to do with a sexual game, it had to be something at the very core of Anthony. I had misunderstood entirely.

When Anthony was 21 his father had found and read his diary in which he had described his belief that he should have been born female. His father confronted him and told him 'stop this nonsense, you are a man, be a man'. In retrospect I see how similar my own reaction was, but at the time, though I was repelled by the cruelty of such a response, I saw no connection. His father had been cruel and selfish, I was just asking for what I had been promised. He was wrong, I was right.

I felt angry and self righteous. One of the things that made me most angry was that in the year before we had met, after his father had died, Anthony had looked on the internet for information about sex change operations. Why hadn't he told me? His answer was quite simply that when we met he believed with not a little relief, that he couldn't be a woman, because he loved me so much and really wanted to spend the rest of his life with me. He had dodged the bullet at the last moment. Meeting me meant he was just a man who liked stockings and all the rest could be packed away and never looked at again. It reminded me of a story I heard about Ghandi in his later life. He admitted to allowing his young female helpers to share his bed in order to 'test his resolve to be celibate'. What, I wondered , happened if he failed? Anthony's belief that he could suppress his feminine self I felt, had been quite a gamble to take with someone else's future.

Unable to say what I wanted without crying or shouting, I wrote Anthony a letter. It explained that though I respected his desire to be a woman, he was not a woman. Furthermore, he was a 6'2" muscular and handsome man and would never be able to look like anything but a bad transvestite, opening himself and those with him to ridicule or worse. What did he think this would do to the children, was he seriously going to turn up to parents evening in heels and lipstick? Though I respected his belief that he was in some invisible sense, female, for all intents and purposes he was male. Tough, get on with it. He could not do this to us. I would not allow him to. I could not have made it plainer the utter lack of support I was offering, but, I said, I still loved him, completely... except for the female bit.

It is not a great letter, it does not cover me in glory. I expect if the transgendered community were giving out supportive family awards, this would not feature. I'm not proud of it and I wish I hadn't written it, but I did. To be fair, over the next few months we both said some pretty awful things to each other.

Afraid as I was of the consequences of Anthony's beliefs, I couldn't help but feel compassion for the man, for the person that I loved. What must it be like to look in the mirror and see the wrong face, the wrong body, the wrong gender? How awful must it be to be rejected again and again, just because you say, 'this is who I really am'? How scary must it be, how desperate must you be to risk loosing your partner, your step children, maybe even all your family and friends, just for admitting your truth? I was pulled violently between this compassion and the desire to keep Anthony unchanged. Within a single hour I would veer wildly between thinking I could accept this and live with Vicky and screaming in my head that I wanted my husband, my Anthony and nothing else. It was exhausting and though I wasn't telling anybody that there was anything wrong, I think the strain began to show. There was no balance in our life anymore, everything was a day to day struggle, a mixture of intense and distressing arguments and housework, paying the bills, life. It was exhausting and miserable, for both of us.

At this very early stage telling no one else about these discussions was part of my strategy. I hoped that I would be able to guide him back to being my husband and no one would ever need to know anything about it. The one person I was talking to was God. I was raised an athiest but had, much as come to think of it, Anthony had described his experience, always been aware of something else that didn't fit that view of the world. I made various exploratory forays into local churches through my teens and finally was baptized in my early twenties. My mother called me the 'white sheep' of the family, but respected my faith, even if it baffled her. So praying had always been a silent part of my adult life.

I found myself in church the next Sunday praying silently for guidance. 'I don't want a hint or a sign or some general sense of well-being' I prayed, 'I want actual guidance, just tell me what to do God, right now, right here', not very polite but to the point. I heard the words in my head, 'Love is the answer'. My voice but not from me. That's how it felt. I knew it was true and it seemed the right piece of information, but a nagging part of me felt much like the recipients of the answer to the question of life the universe and everything in The Hitchhiker's Guide to the Galaxy. Forty-two. Great, wonderful, how do I use that information? How does knowing 'Love is the answer' help me decide what I should do next? Still, it is. I believe, the truth and I've kept that thought with me ever since.

I was determined to maintain the control. Every sign of slight femininity, his longer hair, shirts that looked too blouse like, I would jump on. We had agreed, I would tell him, you won't do that. It has to be private. Nothing that a teenager could pick up on. Nothing. Most days the discussion became a full blown screaming argument. Anthony didn't seem able to understand why I couldn't simply accept who Vicky was. Anthony was just a mask, a cover, not the real person. This was who I had really fallen in love with. If I really loved him, I would love her. If I really loved him. That challenge flew back and forth between us again and again.

We quarrelled again about his hair. I told Anthony it was too long, the time had come to get it cut. Women have short hair too I reasoned, why couldn't he be one of those women? Trouser wearing short haired. I might as well have added beard growing and manly. Anthony was distraught, he couldn't see how such a request was accepting his truth or even trying to accept it. I went on though, determined that I was winning the argument. He looked ridiculous with long hair, and wanting to look like that was ridiculous, he was embarrassing his step-daughter and me. Finally I screamed at him that he was himself ridiculous and selfish and cruel. Anthony ran into the bathroom and I, determined to have the last word, followed him in. He had taken a pair of nail scissors from the bathroom cabinet and he began hacking away at his hair, tears streaming down his face. And I saw it, properly for the first time. At last I understood it. The real agony of this human being. This person that looked like a man, but was, really was at the deepest most important level, a woman. A woman who had spent forty years trying to suppress something that wasn't his fault, no. That wasn't her fault. I recognised the person I loved was in terrible trouble and all I had been thinking was, why is he doing this to me and why won't he stop? I knew that I loved this person, that had never been in doubt, but what I hadn't understood, what I hadn't truly seen until this moment was that at some level at some degree, this person really was as female as me and if I really loved her I had to help her sort herself out.

I cannot imagine what it must be like to be transgendered. It is not imagining how I would feel if I wanted to be a man, it is imagining how I would feel if on the inside I was exactly myself as I am today but had a male body. A body that didn't have anything to do with the real me. I'm female. Everyone who's ever met me knows it, no one questions it. I don't have to do anything to be recognised as female, it just happens. How would it be if everyone told me I was male, reacted to me as male and laughed at me if I suggested otherwise. How would that feel? I don't know but I imagine you'd want the people who loved you to at least believe you. If they really loved you.

I wish I could tell you that I then became a caring and supportive partner and Vicky approached the rest of her journey to become her true self with generosity and compassion, but that really would be a fairytale.

Chapter Two

There are many many different kinds of people on the spectrum of gender. Most of us, sit neatly at either end, male or female. The few thousand left over, and it is only a few thousand who have come out and sought treatment, express a myriad of feelings about their gender. Some are quite clear that their body simply got it wrong. Took a left fork instead of a right somewhere in the womb and delivered the wrong gender body. There are many more male to females than female to males. I don't know why, these things seem to be a combination of genes and hormones and luck. I should make it clear that I am talking only about male to female transexuals, because I'm married to one and those are the transexuals I know. Others find themselves with a random selection of male and female body parts. Some of them may still feel very strongly they are a certain gender, others that they are a third sex, not provided for in the world of form filling, or toilet facilities. Whatever these people experience about gender, everyone I've ever spoken to has been very clear that they knew what they were as soon as they knew what a boy and a girl were. They knew which camp they belonged in and had lived with the dismay and confusion of being put in the wrong one all their lives.

Others feel drawn to express a feminine side whilst utterly sure they are male. I once met a very nice transvestite who had gone the Marilyn Monroe route. When I asked him about his gender he said, I think a little offended, that he was only Marilyn with the clothes and the wig and the make-up, take that away and he was a bloke. Still looked fabulous though! He just liked expressing that part of himself. Vicky, I remember thinking, was Vicky naked. It had nothing to do with what she was wearing. That is not to dismiss the experience of transvestites. Certainly to some it is a sexual thrill and that's an end of it. And why not? Sex should be thrilling. But to many others it is a necessary expression of a real part of themselves. Not all of themselves, but important for their sense of well-being and calm. There is a joke in the transgendered community, it goes: What's the difference between a transvestite and a transexual? Answer: about 4 years. Well, there's some truth in that for some people. Certainly transvestism can be the opening gambit in coming to understand that you are in fact in the wrong gender body, but it's by no means true for all. If you catch your husband in your knickers it's not a foregone conclusion that he is really she. What I have found out over the last few years is, if you want to know someone's gender, ask them, they are the best judge.

Vicky had told me she was Vicky in January 2009. I was still convinced that this would be a long drawn out process and that nobody else was going to need to know anything about it. I still found myself swinging violently between loving support and despairing anger. One moment wondering what life would be like with a woman, and the next fantasizing about escaping and starting a new life on my own away from the inevitable ridicule that would follow a woman who thought she had found her fairytale but had ended up married to a transexual. It was the ridicule and judgement that frightened me, not the actual life. If I had been on a desert island with Vicky, I don't think I would have had a problem.

We did have a problem though. Vicky was miserable. Probably suicidally so if we hadn't done anything, but we did do something, so thank God we didn't have to go down that road. Many transgendered people, unable to square the circle of their reality and what seems possible, do tragically end up committing suicide. Statistically a much higher proportion than the rest of mankind. Some will never have told anyone of their suffering until it's too late. What a sad waste of life, just because it wasn't average.

The first stage, we decided, was that Vicky, I still called her Anthony unless we were alone, should see her G.P and get a referral for psychological assessment. Vicky found out about the clinic which ran out of Charing Cross hospital. It treated Gender Dysphoria, or unhappiness about one's gender. It's an odd term. It covers a very very wide spectrum of people, but some of the people it covers are transexual men and women, who are rather reasonably dysphoric about their apparent gender, as it is mismatched with their actual gender - a thing defined not by a particular set of genitalia, but by their own self-knowledge. It seems odd that such people are treated as having a problem of unhappiness when they have a physical condition. There is, as far as I'm aware, no cancer dysphoria unit. What this comes down to, is funding. Transexuals are treated as having a mental health issue which is resolved with a physical operation. The problem is, the minute you start trying to define a set of physical parameters to describe the condition you will inevitably leave someone on the outside, no longer qualifying for treatment. At least this way no one gets turned away.

Transition is the journey a transgendered person makes to function full time as the gender they know themselves to be, rather than the one that was mistakenly assigned to them at birth. I understood all this, and I never wanted to be the kind of person who would want to stop someone else being themselves. All I can say is, it is different when it's your husband. My vision of this journey was one spread out over decades. Vicky's trip to the doctor's was my first experience of the high speed ride that transition can be. She came back excited, almost euphoric. Her G.P had certainly been taken aback by her request, but had managed after talking to the other doctors at the surgery, to find the correct protocol. As soon as she had had two psychiatric assessments to ensure she wasn't suffering from schizophrenia or some other mental health issue, she could begin hormones and her breasts would begin to grow. A lot of transgendered people feel pretty offended at the suggestion they should undergo psychiatric assessment before accessing the treatment they know perfectly well they need. The trouble is, at this initial stage -gender dysphoria- there are a few people who are genuinely suffering from mental illness, who need other help which has nothing to do with aligning their gender. Obviously it's important to redirect those people to the right treatment for them, but it does have the unwanted side effect of making transgendered people feel as though, once again, they might be 'making it up'. Vicky was just happy and excited to be following the path that would eventually lead to her full physical transition.

I was devastated. No, I was furious. We hadn't even told anyone that she was anything but Anthony, and any minute now Anthony was going to have breasts. Also Vicky said she needed to start living 'in role' dressing as a woman, changing her bank details and driving license to Victoria. This is also a very important part of the transitional journey. Some find the cold hard reality of transition, or living as a woman who looks and sounds like a man, just too hard. Sometimes they start but the reaction and anger of family and friends is just too much to bare. In their fantasy version, transition is the thing that is going to make everything all right. In reality, at least for a time, it adds a huge extra pile of troubles and does nothing to dissipate the ones you came in with. Some people give up at first, but then find that, difficult as it is, and what ever the cost in relationships and painful surgery, they just have to do it. It takes a lot of courage to sort yourself out when you're transgendered.

I told her I needed more time. A lot more time. Well, I may have shouted that actually. I shouted a lot. I felt like I was fighting for my children's happiness, for my world that was crumbling around me at speed. It is easy from the perspective of partner to say, 'wait, not yet, its not the right time' but for the transgendered person who has finally reached the point , after a whole lifetime, of saying 'I can't do this anymore' waiting another half hour is too much.

How long must another few months be for a woman who has been forced to live as a man for 40 years. I got it, really I did, but I truly needed more time to come to terms with this new reality. The strength of her need to move forward and the very real need I felt for more time to understand this shuddered between us like a steel girder about to snap.

Vicky couldn't slow down though, no matter how much I wept and shouted and begged and bullied, no matter how much I said don't do this, the avalanche crashed on. And all through this, we still loved each other and felt lost when the other wasn't there. We were also trying to keep as much normality as we possibly could for the children and for our own sanity. I knew by this time, that I wanted to stay and somehow, somehow make this work. That sounds like a very positive statement, but maybe the more accurate truth is I knew I didn't want to leave and therefore somehow had to make it work. No matter how strange things were, the thought of not being a couple anymore made no sense. I couldn't visualize it. Although some things were changing, other much deeper things were the same and I couldn't and wouldn't walk away from them. Is that, I wonder, how my mother felt when my father's illness changed him so radically just a year into their marriage? In a strange mirror image of my own situation, her husband still looked like himself, though paralyzed down his right side. His mind though was very damaged. My mother sometimes described it as though all his faults and failings had been magnified by the damage to his brain, and which of us could come out of such a process as a tolerable human being? She stayed with him because she refused to believe he was gone, and she loved him. I wanted to stay because I too could not believe the person I had fallen in love with had gone, evaporated. Don't judge a book by it's cover, or as the lovely child of a transgendered women remarked, 'same sweetie, different wrapper'. Intellectually I understood, but my heart was a long way behind.

We hadn't told Ellie yet. I dreaded it, but she had to know what was going on, or one day she would bump into Vicky and that would be a hundred times worse. It was nearly her sixteenth birthday and we agreed we would wait until after that before I would sit down and talk to her. Vicky's euphoria seemed to protect her from the awfulness that was unfolding around her. All she could see was the wonderful prize of freedom just ahead. She felt hurt that I couldn't see how wonderful it was. My distress was disloyal. My requests for her to slow down were unfeeling. If I really loved her then surely I would support her. I felt just as let down, just as confused. Why couldn't she see how hard this was? If she really loved me, she would slow down. Surely she could see how crucial that was. One thing I knew by now though. If I was actually embarking on this journey with Vicky, I couldn't do it alone. I needed someone to talk to, someone who wouldn't be hurt by my inability to rejoice. Eventually everyone would have to be told. That was a huge task ahead and every step off it frightened me, and this was the sort of thing I couldn't believe anyone had ever had to tell anyone before. How on earth do you start such a conversation? I remembered the old joke of the sergeant told to inform a soldier his mother had died. "All those with a mother still living step forward...not so fast Perkins". Maybe I could try, " All those without a transexual sister in law step forward...". Brutal but effective.

The first person I told was my twin sister. We were driving down to visit our dad, who was in a nursing home. After years of very extreme behaviour he had mellowed into a sweet slightly bonkers old man. His speech was not good and he was in a wheelchair. Both these things made him considerably easier to deal with than the mobile talking version. That may sound callous, but trust me, it was an improvement. It was possible to feel closeness, even love for this version of dad. Every now and then he would give you one of his knowing winks that meant, 'you think I don't know but I do'. What he thought I thought he didn't know was part of his own private madness and involved a lot of numbers scribbled on any piece of paper he could lay his hands on. But it didn't matter. Part of his madness was that he didn't seem to know his son was dead. That he was protected from the awful pain of loosing his precious son, was an unexpected side effect of his illness, an illness that had taken so much from him over the years. At least it gave him that. So, driving down to see dad, with my twin sister as captive audience, I chose my moment. I was glad I couldn't look at her as I drove, it was easier to tell her this extraordinary thing without watching her reaction.

I started by saying that recently Anthony had been going through some very tough personal stuff and that we had finally got to the bottom of it. My sister said she had noticed something was up and had wanted to talk to me but I'm such a private person. Well, yes, whatever I imagined about my powers of deception, my sister had been on to that one for years. The moment had come, I'd said there was something up, now I had to say what. 'Anthony is a transexual and he is really a she. She is called Victoria and she is going to transition over the next few years. She told me six months ago and you're the first person I've said a word to.' If I'd been writing for a soap opera, I'd have been sacked for implausible plot lines. My sister was, at first, speechless, then amazed and then very very worried. I focused on the road.

It was a relief to be able to say these things out loud, but it also made it real, in a way it hadn't been just talking to Vicky about it. Now there was no way back. All hope of talking Vicky out of being this, of keeping my life with Anthony, was gone. We talked about the best way to handle this for the whole family. Especially the children and Vicky's mum. My sister was very concerned at the burden this would put on my children, especially as they had both already been through so much. She had hoped it would be plain sailing from here on. I agreed with her, It was all very sensible stuff. We also came up with a time frame for transition. I should ask Vicky to wait until Ellie had left home before she appeared in anything but jeans and a T-shirt. Dressing 'more androgynously' was code for no dresses no lipstick. It was also code for, 'don't actually do this - we'll pretend we accept you as long as you show no signs of being anything but Anthony'. I thought it sounded a terrific plan.

Vicky was very pleased that I had told my sister, but a bit put out that I hadn't told her in advance that's what I was planning. It wasn't the last time that I was to come up against the gap between Vicky's dream of how things would happen and my actions. To be honest though, I hadn't been planning it. The moment was just right so I spoke. Was that selfish? She was my sister after all, but then it was Vicky's condition not mine. I was very attached to being in control of every aspect of our future life together. It was as though I had decided Vicky had forfeit the right to make any decisions by coming out as transgendered. Everything that followed would be as I dictated it, because she owed it to me. She had dropped this huge challenge in my lap and the price for my staying would be a lifetime of doing everything exactly as I wanted.

It wasn't just that this idea would have changed our marriage into punishment and compensation, not a particularly healthy way of life, it would never have worked. That was one of the many dead ends I tried going down before finding the real way forward.

In April, tired of waiting for the NHS to spring into action, Vicky discovered a private clinic in London that could give her the psychiatric assessments she needed, the counselling I wanted her to have and most excitingly from her point of view, the hormones that would get her physical transition under way. This didn't mean she was giving up on the NHS entirely, and at least what she was doing was a lot safer than the route many transgendered people took. The hormones needed for transition and other drugs that promised miraculous effects, were all available through the internet, and some took it upon themselves to self medicate, without any checks or blood tests to see what these hormones were doing to them. It was a dangerous gamble that I am glad Vicky, even at her most impatient, was not tempted to take.

About this time she asked if I would join an online support group for partners of transgendered people. The website was populated by all variations of gender dysphoric people. Transvestites, transexuals, those who felt themselves to be of a third sex, neither wholly male or female, and, I guess, guys who just liked wearing a frock every now and then and wanted to find out where the best thigh length boots size 10 could be found. Reading a few posts very quickly revealed how similar many peoples experience had been to Vicky's. Early childhood awareness seemed the most common factor. Some were out and proud, living their lives fully as women, others dressed secretly when their wives were out, or had already divorced and found themselves in bitter battles to be allowed anywhere near their children. Some were happy, many were suffering great loneliness and anxiety. The posts were on the whole, painfully honest and pretty hard reading.

The partners board was off limits to the transgendered members, the idea being that partners could let off steam and get support from others who had found themselves unexpectedly married to a woman. So I posted:

> *Hi I am Emma, the wife of Victoria C. She's been posting quite a lot on Angels, so I expect some of you know her already. Anyway Victoria told me of her true transgendered nature just over six months ago and of her desire to transition and live as the woman she truly is. I knew Vicky enjoyed cross dressing from almost the beginning of our relationship, and I've always been fine with that, but, the desire to transition was a bit of a surprise (much like hurricane Katrina was a bit windy!).*

It has taken time, lots of discussion, lots of tears, a bit of shouting, but we are still here and heading forward together. We haven't told my two children from my first marriage yet, but we are getting ready to - GCSEs first! So by summertime Vicky will be well and truly 'out'.

I waited a few days and then, there were replies. I was at last in touch with at least one other woman who had been down this path and survived. She was incredibly kind and spoke of so many feelings and fears that I recognised. She was also further down this road than we were. Her partner, she no longer said husband, was getting ready for the final surgery, in which male genitalia would become female.

Let me at this point make one thing clear. In gender reassignment surgery - GCS - NOTHING gets chopped off. OK? I'm sure that any man imagining this process has nightmarish visions of his manhood being lopped off and dumped in a bin. Well that's not what happens. If you are eating, look away now. In the UK this is the most common method. The erectile tissue is removed, the 'tube' is inverted. Nerve endings from the head of the penis form the clitoris. The testes are removed and the skin over them used to create labia. The end result is very convincing. Every effort is made to create a fully functioning vagina, repositioning, but not cutting, the nerves. Sometimes, because everyones body is a bit different, more tissue has to be moved about, and the more you cut and reattach, the greater the risk of tissue rejection. The urethra is also repositioned to allow a more female form of peeing and the end result should be indistinguishable from any other woman's vagina.

It was unexpected to discover that I needed to remind Vicky that most women don't spend their coffee breaks comparing labia size. Another side effect maybe of being raised male, where compare and contrast seems to be the law of the land. I suppose if you've never been in a women only changing room, it's possible you wouldn't be aware of the different atmosphere. Competitive discussions about vagina depth just don't happen. Then again, when most of us discovered our bodies, we were considerably younger and 'you show me yours and I'll show you mine' was quite normal. I'm supportive of Vicky's journey of self discovery, but there, I very much draw the line.

Plenty can go wrong and it will knock you out for months not weeks and you can end up at the end of it all with no sensation at all. Not something one would do on a whim. Not something, really, I think a man would do, but then, a transgendered woman isn't a man. Some transgendered women don't ever have this operation, sometimes because they can't for medical reasons, and sometimes because they don't want to take the risk. They too, are not men.

It was a huge relief to be able to talk about how things were going to someone who understood from the inside. It was also rather worrying to note that this partners board had a membership of about three. If continuing partners of transgendered women ever had a get together, clearly a phone box would be adequate, if not a little roomy.

What had happened to all the other wives? Through the online support groups I had gradually come to see that there were dozens of other women who had married a man who turned out to be a transexual woman. For the most part they formed a huge statistic of sadness. For most of these women the discovery that their partner was transgendered meant, quite suddenly, that they had lost their husband as much as if he had died. Transition meant the very real physical end of their husband and they found themselves married to a woman. They were heterosexual women who suddenly found themselves in a same sex relationship. For the vast majority of them there could be no happy ending. The online forum was full of transgendered women bewailing their wives' unwillingness to change, to 'become' lesbian. It was as unrealistic a dream as a transgendered woman 'becoming' a man, but they didn't seem able to see it. You are what you are. The heart wants what the heart wants. The result was often, but not always broken families. Some couples managed to keep their love and friendship, whilst acknowledging that the physical relationship was over, but I don't think they're a huge group either. It wasn't anyone's fault. I don't think any of these people went into their marriages thinking they would get a nice family set up going and then blow it apart by transitioning. I don't think any of their wives thought, I could be in a same sex relationship, but I won't out of spite. Still, it wasn't hugely encouraging to see the tiny number of transgendered marriages that survived intact. It did make me realize that we were lucky. Vicky hadn't found that she now wanted to be with a man, and I was just as happy to be with a woman. What were the odds of that outcome? Pretty small I think.

Sometimes Vicky and I would go out for the evening to central London, and she would be able to dress up and wear make-up. I found it very very hard. I knew I had to try and get used to this new reality. In theory I would convince myself it was no big deal. If I chose not to be bothered by peoples looks or comments, they would bounce off me. My torments though came from inside myself. I could still see my husband underneath the lipstick. If I held her hand, it was his hand. I found that very difficult and I would sometimes look away so that I could imagine I was still with Anthony, eventually looking back to see Vicky and experiencing the pain of losing 'him' all over again. Why I kept banging my head against that particular brick wall, I can't tell you. I just wasn't ready to let go of 'him' yet, and holding hands was a way of holding on.

I rarely did hold her hand though. She looked every bit the dodgy transvestite and I was just plain embarrassed by her obviously male physique incongruous beneath the floral silk blouse and necklace. Sometimes I would be fine and other times it was unbearable. Once we got ten feet outside the car park and I just froze. It was too much, the feeling that everyone was staring, that people were pointing and laughing. I wanted to be the kind of person who would bravely stand next to Vicky and care nothing for what the world thought. I believed myself to be that kind of person, but I wasn't. I did care. I had loved walking alongside my handsome husband noticing the envious glances of other women. Foolish and childish, but I had loved it. I felt so proud to be his, and now? Now I felt like a freak. Even if Vicky couldn't choose who she was, I had chosen to be with her, and all these strangers were judging me. Well that's how it felt. I'm sure a few people did have a bit of a stare, but so what? I expect I stared at some of them. That's how I feel now. Then I was rooted to the spot with shame and the hideousness of my situation. Vicky was very hurt, why wouldn't she be? I'd encouraged her to dress up, told her she looked lovely, waited until we were in the middle of China town and then bailed on her.

On another occasion we went to a National Trust house for a day out. In my head this was going to be an easy trip. Not in the centre of London, very little risk of bumping into crowds of jeering teenagers. National trust properties do not hold many attractions for teenagers, and if they are there, they are generally so locked in the injustice of their predicament, that they rarely look up. When we got there though I became overwhelmed by embarrassment. It wasn't Vicky's fault, she looked very nice, very unspectacular, but I couldn't walk with her. I strode on ahead consoling myself that no one could tell we were together, let alone, God forbid, a couple. She was desperately hurt. I kept telling her I was staying and supporting her, and yet I only seemed able to stay and pull support from under her at every opportunity. I'm not trying to demonize myself here. I know that I was trying to come to terms with an enormous life change, which most women walk away from on day one. I don't blame them for walking away, and I don't blame me for finding it incredibly hard, I'm just telling you what the consequences were.

Still, practice makes perfect. We continued going out together and gradually got used to going into restaurants and correcting waiters who called her sir. An unexpected problem was that I felt ashamed at being seen as having chosen a transgendered partner. Vicky after all had not chosen to be transgendered. Most people could understand that, but I - I had chosen to be with this person. I wanted people to understand that I had chosen a normal man. THIS had happened afterwards. THIS wasn't my fault. That, I felt was my truth, and if Vicky was going to have her truth recognised then me too thank you very much. Public spaces were a very stressful experience for me in that first year. If we could have just never gone out again I would have been happier.

Sometimes I would find the staring particularly hard because people would wait until Vicky's back was turned and then point and laugh. It didn't seem to matter that I was looking directly at them. For some reason petrol stations were particularly bad. I remember as Vicky walked back to the car, having paid inside the shop, the cashier called the other staff over to the window and they stood and laughed with no idea of the hurt they were causing. Well with no concern for the hurt they were causing anyway.

I'm sure people, particularly teenagers, don't spend much time considering the pain they cause pointing out someone's difference. I experienced it with my son, with people making audible comments and tutting when his behaviour didn't conform. Now I was experiencing it with Vicky. To be honest I was getting a bit tired of turning the other cheek.

I amaze myself looking back at this time how very much I cared what people thought. I had always seen myself as someone who accepted the rainbow variety of humanity. I had gay friends but beyond condemning homophobia, I didn't give much thought to what their lives might be like day to day. Did they have to put up with comments from narrow minded strangers. Did they get 'spotted' the fact that they were a couple. Never? Sometimes? What must that be like? To be regarded as odd just for being yourself. I had no idea, well, I'd had no idea. I was beginning to find out. Before this though, I had intellectually supported anyone's right to express their sexual orientation, but at the same time enjoyed the benefits of being half of a heterosexual couple in a heterosexual society. Booking a hotel room, going to a party where we didn't know anyone, walking together around the supermarket. I had never had to question my right to do those things unmolested. Big companies are certainly more switched on than small ones. Individuals put in a situation where they could ask you questions, wanted to ask questions. Most people were surprisingly kind. Well I was surprised anyway. The vast majority of people who weren't, were young, foolish and usually drunk. Not exactly a cross-section of society.

Drunk men and women are far more likely, when in the protective cover of a group, to shout out abuse or point and laugh loudly. I hated walking past pubs. The truth is though, Vicky was at far more risk when she was out on her own. My presence, as a 'normal' person, seemed to signal to other people that Vicky was not a 'wierdo', but a normal person too. When she was on her own she suffered far more verbal abuse than she ever did with me.

One aspect of Vicky going out on her own surprised me. She was rather worryingly unaware of the dangers that a single woman might face late at night on her own. I suppose these are the things mothers teach their little girls and don't mention to their little boys. Being conditioned to be male Vicky had never had to think in this way and responded to my anxious warnings like a stroppy teenager convinced that such dangers were the fevered imaginings of the over-protective. Vicky though, for all her plucked eyebrows and nail polish, still had the strength of Anthony. It would have been an unwise mugger who attacked her.

I wondered what it was about her that was so threatening. Partly, I think it is the misunderstanding that cross-dressing is always, always sexual and parading about in public is forcing your private sexual desires onto strangers. Following on from that misapprehension is the idea that a transexual, even if they have undergone every surgery available to make them look naturally female, is perceived as a really committed transvestite who has just gone that little bit further to 'get the look'. There is not much public understanding of the inner life of a transexual. When we were together though I was always quick to leap to her defense. My public support of her, if challenged, was much better than my private support, undermined as it was by so many fears and reservations.

For all these reasons then, holding hands was very difficult for me at. We had always held hands and cuddled in public without a shred of embarrassment. A greeting hug at the airport or a farewell kiss, All these things were natural and acceptable from a heterosexual couple in a heterosexual society. Now I mostly refused to hold her hand. Anything more was unthinkable. I didn't want anyone to know the nature of our relationship. I was Vicky's friend. Her kind accepting heterosexual friend. No one need judge me. She would try to take my hand and I would pull away. I would take her arm but after a few moments give it back. I absolutely would not kiss her in public. Not on the lips, not on the cheek. No kissing. People would stare. Maybe they would attack. I was very afraid. Kissing and holding hands in public were just two of the things I was loosing. Vicky was absolutely unable to see that I was loosing anything. Why, she wondered, couldn't I just hold hands and kiss her in public. Easy. She could not contemplate the idea that her transition was taking anything from me. She couldn't understand why I didn't want to call her my wife. She could not see that I had been the wife, the only wife, and she had been the husband. Bacon and Eggs, Beans and Toast, Husband and Wife. I didn't want to be wife. I had been wife to Anthony. I was not Vicky's wife and she was not mine. Some people were happy to call each other wife she told me. That's nice, I thought, I'm not one of them.

Vicky was determined that nothing essential was changing and that I was being stubborn in refusing to move swiftly to happily ever after. What was the big deal? She was the same person I had married, it was still the same. Well, some bits were the same, but some very important bits weren't. Sometimes I thought I was going mad, because what seemed so reasonable and obvious to me, was utter nonsense to Vicky. Our discussions always became painful and angry. We always shouted. We didn't really get any further forward. There was just so much pain on both sides. I couldn't see how we would ever get beyond this. It was a time of great misery, but because we had only told my sister up to this point, and more importantly, not the children, we were still trying to maintain the illusion of business of usual. Running a normal happy family for the sake of the children sounds such a good idea, but who is a good enough actor, or so detached from their feelings that they can really successfully pull it off?

We decided we needed to do something fun. Vicky was very keen to see 'Priscilla Queen of the Desert', the stage musical based on the australian film. The story revolves around a drag queen going to meet his son for the first time. His fears about how that meeting will go, and whether or not his son will accept him. It definitely struck a chord with us as we got closer to telling Ellie. The show was of course, wonderful. More feathers and crazy costumes per square foot than the House of Lords. In between all that though, It was surprisingly moving. When we got outside the theatre Vicky suddenly pulled me to one side, collapsed into my arms and sobbed her heart out. All the fear about how Ellie might react just hit her, in the middle of Cambridge circus. As I hugged her and listened to her talking about this enormous weight of emotion I thought 'Thank God, now we can move forward together'. Finally I felt she was facing her fears as well as her hopes. Before this I had felt like the bad part of good cop bad cop, with me delivering all the negative stuff and Vicky in danger of turning into Julie Andrews and bursting into a rousing chorus of 'my favourite things'.

It was something of a breakthrough. I also began to understand that part of my struggle was caused by trying to move and stay in the same place all at the same time. There were only two ways forward. Stay and embrace the person Vicky was or accept I couldn't and leave. I had been trying to do both, everyday I was questioning whether I could accept this but not deciding and neither staying nor leaving. It wasn't fair to Vicky and it wasn't fair to me. My body, stuck on the treadmill of my indecision, had rewarded me with coughs and colds and niggling sore throats that just wouldn't go away. I knew I had to make my mind up and get on with it. I knew it but I found it very hard to actually do. I would think to myself, yes, I have made my decision, I'm staying, I can live like this and then minutes later be overwhelmed with fear. How could I possibly stay, how could I put my children through this. I found myself getting through the most difficult bits by telling myself that I was probably going to leave. I would call her Vicky and then in my head say 'Anthony, Anthony Anthony'. Even if no one would know, I would secretly hang on to him. It was fairly nuts and the truth was I didn't even mean it anymore. I knew Vicky was the real person she had always existed, with a top layer of Anthony, and I had fallen in love with all of him and that meant I had fallen in love with her. I didn't want a life without her. This was the process of letting Anthony go. It wasn't going to be done anywhere but in my head and it was going to be done alone. The choice was not Anthony or Vicky. The choice was let go of Anthony or leave, so at last, I began to let go.

My mood by the end of May 2009 was broadly hopeful. I felt I was getting to grips with life and that I would be able to control the telling of the children at the right time, a time which I would decide. I was still regularly entering into discussions online, sometimes with partners but more often with transgendered women. I wanted to be a voice they might hear from the other side of the fence that they might get a glimpse at how it felt being the partner.

> *One of the biggest issues any mother will struggle with is causing their child pain. when they're new born you won't let anyone with a cold near them, believing that with good enough care they will never get sick, never graze their knee, never hear an unkind word. This is called a 'new' parent. It passes. Thinking about asking my children to take on this challenge, I couldn't help remembering my own journey thus far and wanting to protect them from it. The inner mother tiger engaged. I had to remind myself that challenge was not all bad. A person who never had a cold has no immune system built up. A person who has never been challenged has no idea how to cope with life.*

Now we were moving forward together, in a more realistic way. I felt, for the first time in a long time, like we were a couple again. I was still very anxious about telling the children but, I trusted them to be the people I knew them to be. Not telling them wasn't an option... eventually they would notice the tall dark woman at the breakfast table.

Chapter Three

It was six months since the night in January when Anthony had told me she was Vicky. It was also a week since Ellie's sixteenth birthday and there was no more putting it off. I had to tell her what was going on. As I walked up the stairs to her room I felt exactly as I had done on the night I had had to phone my mother and tell her that my brother, her only son, had been killed on his motorcycle on the M40. He had been knocked off by a driver who had pulled out without looking. The driver was later shown to have been on his mobile phone. Whether or not he had been drinking was impossible to prove, because he drove away from the scene and only handed himself in three days later when any trace of alcohol would have been long gone anyway. Maybe he hadn't been drinking, it makes little difference. It wouldn't have made my brother any less dead. My only knowledge of this man is that he, like my brother, had two small boys at the time, so whatever penalties the law exacted, he knows that two boys grew up without their father because of him.

On the night my brother died it was me who had to call my mother and tell her this thing that would ruin her life. Before I told her she existed in a state in which her beloved son was alive, even though he had been dead for several hours by the time I spoke to her. Once I spoke, that reality, false as it was, was destroyed. Now climbing up to Ellie's room I felt the same. If I didn't say anything, maybe left it until tomorrow or next week, she could have more time believing that she had a step-father who would always be there. I was about to take all that away from her and ask her to embark on a journey that I hadn't yet worked out myself. I had no idea where this was going, was it even possible, had anyone ever done this before, yet I wanted her to accept all this uncertainty in exchange for a life that had for the last six years, been very happy.

I was also, and I was acutely conscious of this, asking her to understand me in a new way. I was a woman who was going to have another woman as a partner. I was telling her I was OK with that. How would she feel? Did it matter to her that I should be a run of the mill heterosexual. Was telling her this tantamount to sharing descriptions of my sex life? What teenager wants that?! I was terrified that not only would she reject Vicky for being Vicky, but that she would reject me for staying with Vicky. How would that affect her own relationships in the future, and what undoable damage was I about to do? I'm amazed I made it to the top of the stairs.

I have always been very close to both my children, but the time spent with Ellie after my divorce, when we were struggling to make ends meet, had been strangely wonderful. Though in practical terms it had been a slog, it had also been just the two of us, while her brother was away at school. Being the sibling of a disabled child as I have said, can be very disabling. I could at last, put her first. Do the things she wanted to. She could have sleep overs and parties. If she needed picking up from somewhere I could just go get her. She often told me I was the kind of mother she could talk to, tell anything too. I was not like other mothers, like her friends mothers. I was cool. I felt very proud and very lucky. My relationship with her was the jewel in my emotional crown. The thought of risking it, of loosing it, was terrifying.

But there was no possibility of not telling her. She was already aware something was up with her step-father. I wasn't the only one who had been living with the stressed and distressed person who had stopped smiling and withdrawn into silence. When I started to tell her that I now knew what his problem was, she told me she had wondered if he was a drug addict. Schools are very up on telling their charges the warning signs of drug addiction and, with the evidence she had it wasn't a bad guess.

I sat on the end of her bed and said I had something important to discuss. I told her that there was a very rare medical condition that Anthony had been born with and though It wasn't going to kill him it was going to change him. I explained that Anthony was transgendered. This meant he hadn't been born entirely male. In his case his brain was female and his body male. It had made him very unhappy because he loved us all very very much but he couldn't go on pretending to be male when he was really female. She cried, she asked did that mean I was a lesbian, she asked if her step dad wanted to go all the way to become a woman, she asked who was going to walk her down the aisle. She asked lots of sensible questions but I could see how shocked she was. It was every bit as painful as I had feared.

She said she was very shaken. She also said that she still loved her step-dad and didn't want him to move out, neither did she for that matter. She just wanted to give him a hug and not talk about it with him yet, and then she would like to go out with me and not be in the house for a while. I felt desperately sorry to have caused her so much distress, but also so proud that she had reacted with such maturity and kindness. This was going to take time to get used to, of course it was, but she was willing to try. She was willing to reach out with compassion to Vicky.

I left her to get ready to go and stay with a friend, a friend who would of course be told nothing about this, and went downstairs feeling not a little relieved that the ground hadn't crumbled beneath me and that my daughter still wanted us to be a family. It was a pretty good outcome all things considered. I really believed at that moment that the worst was over.

What I had completely failed to consider was how Vicky would feel, discovering this seismic moment in our family's life had taken place without warning and without her involvement. I was very clear in my mind that telling Ellie without Vicky in the room was essential. If she had needed to scream abuse and anger and hatred, if that were her reaction, better by far that Vicky didn't have to take it. I would protect my child, giving her the space to feel however she felt, and I would protect Vicky. How marvelous I was.

That was not how Vicky saw it. She was outraged that I hadn't even warned her that I was going upstairs to do this momentous thing, she thought I was putting some clothes away. I was I have to admit, staggered by her reaction. I had been expecting praise and thanks for my delicate handling of the situation, even rejoicing that Ellie said she still loved Vicky. Amazing, I thought, wonderful. Vicky was furious saying I had presented it all wrong and given Ellie a negative spin on everything. Had Vicky been the one to tell instead of me, then all, she maintained, would have been smiles and laughter. She screamed at me and I screamed at her. The pain was palpable and unstoppable. In retrospect, this was the moment the bubble burst. My bubble that we could all get through this calmly with logical mutually supportive chats which I would control, and Vicky's bubble that she could control other people's reactions and move smoothly and swiftly to a life virtually unaltered by her transition. Actually, bubble bursting is entirely the wrong term. I should say, this is when the volcano erupted. I was definitely standing too close.

I vented my anger in the partners forum online:

> *I don't think I have ever felt so let down by her. I put myself and my relationship with my Ellie on the line today. Vicky told me my relationship with my Ellie was never under any threat, why was I worried etc etc etc. I gasp at her naivety. I told our Ellie Vicky and I were staying together, and yes that would make us a lesbian couple. I tried to explain why Vicky hadn't been straight about who she was from the*

beginning. I did everything I could to present this without bringing an agenda to it. My Ellie was upset, confused and angry with both of us at times. She said she had already dealt with a lot of hard stuff in her life and didn't want any more 'difference'. I listened. I hugged her. It was very hard for me seeing my child distressed and not being able to take that away.

If we are to survive as a family, Vicky is going to have to take her share of responsibility for what's happening, and not just become angry with me for failing to wave a magic wand. Today after months of preparation and discussion, when it came to the crunch Vicky let me down. That may take a while to get over.

While Ellie was staying with her friends I decided it was time to tell my mum what was going on. this time I let Vicky know before I spoke to her. At least for me this time of telling the astonishing truth was no longer the first time, and I think each subsequent time of telling someone, 'you know Anthony, well, she's a woman', got easier.

My mum, concert pianist, survivor of being married to my dad, novelist, Russian translator of note and introducer of bread and butter pudding to the Soviet Union, is not your average mum. She brought her phenomenal logical brain to bear on much of the nonsense she'd been brought up with, racism, homophobia, narrow-mindedness of all kinds. I knew that whatever her reaction would be, it would not be based on any kind of prejudice.

She was worried for us all, of course, but included in her worry was Vicky. How hard it must have been living with this for forty years, how much courage it must have taken to come out with it at last. She wanted to come round and meet her. So we did, and she gave Vicky a big hug. Online I posted:

My mum is THE BEST :-) I told her earlier today. I think this is the dream reaction for any TG from a mother in law. She said she would never have guessed this was the problem, but as it was, it must have been so so hard for Vicky and she thought I was wonderful for staying with her, that must be true love. She was worried for Vicky because she knew how much she would have to go through but she thought it was wonderful that she had reached this point and she (my mum) was there for her.

That day, the day I told Ellie about Vicky had been the 'end of the beginning'. I had foolishly imagined we had climbed the mountain and reached the peak. We had of course just run smack into the actual mountain. I was going to need more sherpas.

We limped on for a week, with Ellie at her friends and Vicky and I locked in interminable conversations that descended into weeping and shouting on an hourly basis.

I know that Vicky is going through hell. I know she wants so many things she hasn't got yet and is fearful of so many things that may happen. I even understand that her shouting outbursts are born of fear and distress and are not meant to hurt me. BUT. They do hurt me and there is a finite amount of that I can handle, being only human and all.

There is so much love and acceptance for Vicky and me, I hope she can get to a point where she can benefit from it.

As for Ellie, she is coming home tonight, she doesn't want to talk yet. I know Vicky will find that hard and even hurtful, but I really hope she manages to take it calmly because otherwise we will have trouble.

It's hard to look back at that time. Until then, we had been managing to some degree. It felt like we would calmly talk our way through any problems, and somehow come through to a happy living situation without tearing our lives apart. Telling Ellie was the beginning of the breakdown. First of all it was a personal breakdown for Vicky. The floodgates of pain and a lifetime of pent up rage were unleashed in her disappointment. It was inevitable I think. There was no way that Ellie could have reacted that would have lived up to the fantasy in Vicky's head. Up until that moment she had been living in a state of euphoria, genuinely unafraid of the possible negative outcomes because the prize was so big and shiny it just blinded her to everything else. The sad truth is though, you cannot break free from forty years of living a concealed life without a big explosion and the time for Vicky's big explosion had arrived.

The second breakdown was my own. My fantasy that I could handle everyone and keep everything jogging along without disruption was exploded, and in that explosion my grief at the loss of my husband welled up. Though no one had died, there was real loss. I was bereaved. My husband was gone and yet I could still hear his voice, hold his hand. But it was not his voice and it was not his hand, they were Vicky's. What the hell had happened? Where did my husband go? Where did my happiness go and what in God's name was I going to do now? It wasn't just the loss of my husband and all that middle of the road normality. It was the loss of a life that was fun, that I had allowed myself to get used to. My expectations had been drastically altered when I met Anthony and I had allowed my guard to drop.

Before him, my experience had been that life was pretty hard and lots of unexpected but awful things will knock you down regularly. Your job is to get up, keep smiling and be strong enough to stop any of that rubbish getting your children. In that you could be proud and hold your head up even if you couldn't afford holidays or bicycles.

Anthony taught me how to be wrapped up and protected in his love, I stopped fearing and started trusting. I felt like this had been a huge mistake.

When Ellie was out of the house I no longer felt obliged to stay in the same building as Vicky. The anger and pain that was erupting out of every pore of her was unbearable, and at that point, being very squarely laid at my door. There was no compassion left in me, just anger and indignation. I left. I had no idea if I was going to my sister's house for a cup of tea or to stay until I could find a new life. I was utterly shattered and only able to think of that exact moment.

My sister was sad but not surprised to see me. She was horrified to hear how badly Vicky continued to react. I just couldn't stop crying, it was unbearable pain, could I really have just lost the love of my life. Really? Forever? How had we got to this? What the hell just happened? We all want unconditional sympathy and dogged partisan support at moments like that, but I'm not sure how good it is for us. Surrounded by people who kept telling me how marvelous I was and how dreadful Vicky was, I was all too willing to listen. On the other hand I can't imagine I would have reacted well if they'd all told me how marvelous Vicky was and what a terrible wife I was for leaving, so I can't really blame anyone but myself for buying into words that were meant to soothe and comfort but which I took as objective truth.

Vicky tried to call me and she sent texts but I wouldn't reply. Instead I sought more support from the partners online, the only people I felt, who might have the slightest idea what was going on.

I posted, where Vicky would not be able to read or comment:

The thing is, I thought it did go well! I thought Ellie took it really well!! She was saying she still loved her step dad, understood this wasn't something he was doing but something that was happening and she even went down and gave him a hug!!!! I mean, God knows what Vicky was expecting, but I think that was pretty damn marvelous of her.

Since then all I've had is a list of my 'failures' to make this all easy and happy. I'm gobsmacked!!!!!! I can't believe, after all the support I have given, after the huge journey I have made to understand that I love Vicky and we can be together as two women, after all that, to be told that I'm letting Vicky down? All she seems able to give me is anger and resentment - I just don't know how to move beyond that.

I thought our marriage was secure and I trusted she loved me, but I really don't know now. Maybe, despite all her protestations, she doesn't want to stay together and is sub consciously driving me away? My daughter has gone to stay with her friends, I know she's told her closest friend what's going on, so at least she's not dealing with this on her own, but I wanted to be there for her, instead of which I'm at my sisters house trying to decide what on earth to do.

One last thing, both my daughter and my niece, who is 19, had assumed from Vicky's behaviour over the last few months, that she was on drugs, such has been the change in her personality from happy and fun to angry and grumpy most of the time. Vicky still won't acknowledge she's angry - she says its all me 'over reacting' but how many people will it take for her to question her own behaviour and stop 'lashing out' at those around her.

Honestly, I'm devastated, because I don't want to lose Vicky, but right now I see no way forward

Vicky's refusal to agree that she was angry or behaving in any way unreasonably was an aspect of the arguments that I found particularly difficult to deal with. For me that refusal hit a lot of very sensitive triggers from my childhood. My father, irrational and often violent lurked in my memory. His rages, sometimes connected to epileptic seizures and sometimes not, were terrifying to us as children. Almost worse though, was his ability to switch them off suddenly, leaving us near hysterical with distress while he told us to 'calm down'. I can barely type those two words. 'calm down'. Saying them out loud still makes me feel mildly nauseous.

The echo of this childhood experience in Vicky's insistence that she was not angry but simply making a valid point, when she had been screaming at me, made it unlikely I would respond well. Instead I froze inside. "This is madness' I would think, 'I've seen this before and I'm not going through it again'. It made me want to run and run and never look back. Except that there was a part of me that understood this was not the same as my father's madness, this was just failing to deal with an enormous amount of emotion all released at once. The reaction was, at some level, reasonable. If this had happened to me, I would think, I expect I'd be screaming. I wanted to help her, I just didn't want to be screamed at while I was doing it.

It was an awful time and it ended with all three of us in different places. Ellie at her friends, Vicky at home, fuming, and me at my sisters. That didn't even last the whole evening though, because I couldn't stay away. My sister wanted me to stay the night. Everything was calm and normal there, I could have supper with them, relax, and have some space to decide what I should do. It was eminently sensible and very tempting but I just couldn't do it. I went home. We needed to keep talking, and somehow find a way through this mess. The thought that such anger could end in us being in separate places made it feel like the path to never being in the same place again. I didn't want that, even after all the shouting, I still wanted my soul mate.

The next few days were really unhappy. We just didn't seem to be able to get more than a few sentences into a discussion before both of us ended up shouting or weeping. Neither of us could leave it alone, I don't know if it was deep love or deep stubbornness, but we just couldn't stop. The power of Vicky's distress felt like a physical attack and she seemed to find my tears equally aggressive as though I wept them to control her. I was relieved that Ellie was still staying with friends. What they must have thought was going on I don't know. Being away from it all though, I think she found herself in the same position I had been in months earlier. As long as she didn't tell anyone, this wasn't happening, and maybe if she didn't tell anyone for long enough, it wouldn't happen at all. She stayed away for a week, but then she came back and tried, as much as possible, to stay out of Vicky's way.

I found myself spending more time at my sisters as I tried to avoid the worst of the storm, mostly in tears and always utterly lost as to what to do. One evening my mother, with her typical gallows wit, even managed to make me laugh by saying, "Really Vicky this is no time to start behaving like a man".

Both Vicky and I used the online support group as a way not only to off-load our pain, but also to communicate with each other when talking was just impossible.

> *I don't know why Vicky hasn't posted here yet. She is very unhappy today and we are not in the same space.*
>
> *She tried to have a normal conversation with Ellie this morning and Ellie was typical monosyllabic teenager - still she did talk, so yay.*
>
> *It seems that any perceived slight at the moment unleashes the torrent of misery inside Vicky. Luckily not at*

Ellie but at me. Things like 'am I a monster or a leper?'
Should I be invisible now? Is Ellie allowed to be a brat and
I just have to take it?' etc etc etc.

I understand these are Vicky's big fears. But she's
dumping them all on Ellie saying Ellie doesn't care about
her because she's not behaving as Vicky would like.

I just sent her a text saying - 'you are on the Titanic
arguing about who gets to steer. We are sinking do
something.'

And why I am saying this Vicky you doughnut, is
because I LOVE YOU. Time to move forward.

Everyone else, wish us luck, I think we need it

Vicky also posted, but of course I could read what she was saying. I felt annoyed that private arguments had suddenly become the subject of an online discussion, but we were both posting things and both just trying to get heard and understood. I have to say, many of the trans-women on the site spent a lot of time telling Vicky how lucky she was to have a partner at all and, to put it politely, not to blow it. There's no question though that they understood far better than I or any other non-transgendered person could, what she was going through, and their posts were generally kind and supportive.

It was at this point that the partner of another transgendered woman offered Vicky a much needed outside perspective. She had so far been an enormous help to me in coming to terms with the truth of what had happened, now she firmly but kindly told Vicky the view from there.

Vicky

How long have you had to come to terms with your
situation? How long has Emma had? Ellie is still coming

to terms and until she does (and that may not be a good outcome for you but it sure as hell won't be if you don't back off) she is struggling to maintain being her version of civil to you.

Other significant others log onto sites and electronic scream and shout and do the woe is me line to each other and then realise that the other SOs are saying 'hang on - think about this'. Your step-Ellie does not have that facility and in caring for you she is not wanting to engage in a discussion with you that might hurt your feelings when in the fullness of time (there's that word again) she could actually have a conversation with you where she talks of ordinary everyday life and things pertinent to your transition without any heat or pain but just talks and you say where you are, Emma says where she is and Ellie finds her place within that.

You cannot say I did not warn you that teenagers are a breed apart and there way of dealing is not always conducive to happy family life (this is not solely related to trans issues either) and I would also remind you of all the things she has not done or said but you seem hell bent on deciding that is what she is thinking. I am beginning to see why my partner gets so cross with me when I tell her I know why she is doing something when it is not her intention at all.

Please take a moment to realize that although Emma would not have taken this behaviour from her Ellie on other occasions this is not like other occasions at all - My partner had got to the stage where she HAD to transition whatever the cost - this meant she knew what it could cost her and realized what she was asking from her family. I have asked you before to consider your step-Ellie's lack of male role models and I would ask you again - she is in *turmoil and in not wanting to cause you any pain (through love!!) she is choosing to not discuss anything until she has it in perspective from all angles - which is why she has talked to her peers and close family. She is probably feeling guilty too that she cannot come to terms with it straight away as she thinks her mother and those close family members have done.*

You made me so happy that you were able to take it one day at a time and now you going back on that and cannot even take it one hour at a time.

Your mention of finances is particularly cruel btw - so you would want your family's love and support in exchange for the comforts you provide? What does that sound like?

Please read back what you have written in recent posts and realize you are close to meltdown and for your own sake seek help?

I said before blast at me if you think it will help not at your family.

That evening I tried again

Sweetheart. You lied to yourself and us that you didn't need to be a woman. That's ok. I understand why. Ellie doesn't YET. Give her time. She loves you, she is trying to work this out. Is she worth it? I think so.

Cross dressing is not being transexual - this site testifies to the number of people who love to show off their feminine side but happily identify their gender as male. It's a different thing. Nothing to be ashamed of, but different.

So, in order to move forward, WAIT. I know it's painful and difficult, but you are strong,and at the end of this you will get to be a transgendered woman with a loving wife and daughter. Lucky you! Hands up all those who would like to be in Vicky's position?

You said, "Years ago... I sometimes used to say to my dad "I love you". Sometimes he would reply "Hmmmm. That's just mouth. Don't tell me, show me."

Wow - and yet you have managed to be a loving and gentle parent to your step-daughter. Well done darling, the odds were stacked against you but you didn't become your father.

At the end of each traumatic day, we still ended up in the same bed, arms wrapped round each other saying 'I love you'. I kept thinking, 'Look how bad it got, look how hard it was'. It had been for both Vicky and for me, but we were working it out. We both got very very upset, but we just kept talking or texting or even just posting online until we were ready to be in the same space and listen to each other.

It was painful stuff, but the rule we tried to stick to was, NEVER go to sleep on a quarrel. We were both trying to keep to that rule. Sometimes it was hard, near impossible to go back to the fray and try again to have a conversation, but at some point the love would win through because it's stronger than all the rest.

This was base camp, level one. We had stopped shouting, for the moment. There was still a lot of pain but both of us were trying to remember why we wanted to be together, rather than what was blowing us apart. I couldn't even begin to imagine the future stages of transition, what trauma was heading our way, but we had got through part one and whatever else might happen, we never had to do that bit again. It was a shock to look back over the last six months and compare it to the years before that, when everything had seemed so easy. I remembered my maisonette with the rotting shag pile carpet. Yes we were a mess and would need a lot of work to make us a family again, but we, got to be ourselves, all the time. It would be better to pull the wallpaper off if there was mould underneath, it was the only way it would ever get better.

A few weeks after the initial explosion, when I had told Ellie about Vicky, Vicky wrote a letter to Ellie and left it in her room for her to read. Despite her desperate desire to talk to Ellie face to face, she could see this might be a gentler way to start a conversation.

Dear Ellie,

I thought I would write you a letter because it might be easier to share with you some of the answers to the questions I imagine you have. I am guessing you have lots of questions about this, if someone told me what you were told on Monday then I would have a lot of questions.

It actually has occurred to me that you have experienced an event that has major implications on your life and I want to help you understand that even though this event is happening, I still want to keep life as normal for you as I can.

You are a beautiful, intelligent, smart, feisty independent young woman and I am more proud than you can imagine of you. I love you very much.

Maybe because of that, this letter still feels like a scary thing for me to write. Anyway, I'm not getting to explain myself... so onward. I can guess some of the questions you might have but even then I don't know what order those questions are in inside your head, so I just want to share with you some of my story and I hope that that answers some of your questions and that you might then feel you are able to ask me others. If you don't want to ask me questions then that's OK but I will do my best to answer any question you think of that you feel able to ask.

One of the things I thought you might wonder was how did I come to think or know I was a female in a man's body.

Well done if you are still reading at this potentially embarrassing moment.

I first got an idea that I might be wrong when I was a child (about 5, 6, 7 years old) and I did not look like the girls I was playing with - I was surrounded by girls as a child. Aside from my two friends, the neighbours I had on each side of my house and opposite (and I used to play with all of them) were all girls and it confused me that I seemed to be quite different from them.

I kept my wonderings secret apart from telling one best friend from primary school, it wasn't a big deal to him but he knew. When he moved when I was about 14, it just became my secret until I started going out with my first girlfriend when I was 17.

...I guess that was one of my problems. Back then (like now) I wanted to tell the person I "fell in love with" and that was my first experience of how much I could get hurt by sharing a secret. Its been one of my big sufferings - people that I felt close to getting to know about this part of me and then deciding that they did not want to have anything to do with me once they knew. Even my Dad, when he learnt about the feelings I had (when I was 21) told me he thought I was a freak.

But the questions and fear I felt about myself never went away.

Another thing I was not sure about, in fact made me think that I was completely wrong about my inner feelings was that I have always been attracted to women and so I thought IF I like women and not men, then surely I must BE a man and not a woman.

All the same even though I have constantly wondered if I am a woman with the wrong body, I never got to the point till now where I was brave enough to ask for medical help.

One of the things I have learnt about myself is that whatever I look like on the outside, the inner me has always been the same person and will pretty much stay that way even after changing the outside appearance. The person you already know me as, may change a bit but only because I will be more relaxed and comfortable in who I am. Hopefully you will find me easier to get along with!

I understand that you might look at my denial or fear to speak up as me lying - I get that. I am sorry I did not have the courage to talk to you sooner about this or get the medical help I need and I am now being offered.

I am sorry for the hurt I have caused you.

This is a long process and at the moment all I have actually done is speak to two Doctors one of which is a specialist in gender issues and I have also had about 6 hours of therapy sessions with two different Therapists - both specialists in gender issues.

For the time being, I am continuing to see those same Doctors and Therapists.

I understand how important fitting in with your peer group is at your age and I am not seeking to cause you unnecessary embarrassment.

Also I understand if you prefer that I do not come in person to your school, but try and remember this is a diagnosed medical condition and I cannot choose not to have it.

Well I guess I have said all I can think of at this moment.
All my love

Vicky so wanted her step-daughter to understand her, to know that even if Vicky looked really different from Anthony, that person who wanted to hear what she had to say, who cared what she thought and wanted every wonderful thing that life had to offer for her, was still there. He hadn't gone, he was just female. Vicky wanted to give everything to her step-child, except time. She had no patience to wait while there was a journey towards understanding, and the longer she waited the less she trusted that journey was even going on. Her fear that maybe their relationship was lost was the most destructive emotion she possessed.

I had, at the end of that most difficult week, the week I told Ellie and everything fell apart, found myself offering advice to a transgendered woman who was struggling to understand her wife's 'lack of support'. As I wrote I began to make sense of my own feelings :

> *A thought struck me - when Vicky first told me about her true self, my reaction was very like your wife's. I effectively said, ok, this is who you are but the children must never know, or at least not until they're adult. In other words I bargained. You may be this only if you do it my way.*
>
> *As we went on, Vicky became more and more unhappy because what I was saying was - what you are is shameful and will hurt the children - you must hide away. Not fair and not do-able.*
>
> *I think this bargaining is part of that well known process (which I will now doubtless quote incorrectly!):*

Shock. Denial. Anger. Bargaining. Depression. Acceptance. It applies to bereavement but I have found myself going through that same process with Vicky's transition. My first reaction was a sort of disbelief, followed by the feeling that I could demand how it would pan out. My 'bargaining' You can be you but only when I say so. which leads of course, to anger and depression, except I've never been one for depression - (both parent's and a son who have at one time or another suffered with that I somehow dodged that particular bullet)

So now I am at acceptance, which is a jolly nice place to be if you can get there. I would want to say to anyone who thought they could control another person's self expression, even to protect their children - and as one who tried - it can't be done, and in the end it shouldn't be done. That way madness lies.

"Now I am at acceptance". You've got to admire my optimism really. I think I may have genuinely believed I was now the 'done deal'. I had come to terms with my partner being a transgendered woman and could at last move smoothly on with the rest of our life together. There were no more emotional skeletons in my cupboard and no ghosts in the machine of my reconstruction. She hadn't even started hormone treatment yet, and I thought I had the whole thing under control. Altogether now, 'Ha'.

Chapter Four

After the week of shouting and weeping I had come up with a good idea. It was self defense but it was also a genuine attempt to help Vicky say what she needed. It was certainly a better plan than shouting at each other from dawn to dusk. These were the rules, and I wrote about them online in case someone else was going through the same thing, because they actually helped.

I am trying to put some ground rules in place to avoid a repeat of the last week, which frankly has been hell.

If I start crying or Vicky starts shouting, the conversation ends. The distressed person has to deal with their distress before we do anything else. If no other support can be contacted fast enough Vicky is to call Samaritans.

There is to be a family agreement that whatever else we don't feel able to give each other, we will always give kindness. We won't ignore each other or dismiss each other's feelings

Compared to yesterday's conversations I would say it worked. A couple of times Vicky began shouting and I just said, 'Right we will have to continue this conversation when you feel able to. She struggled, but she did it, and because we weren't just trading pain, we got through and managed to discuss what needed to be discussed. Right now I'll take that as success.

Vicky has apologized for hurting me, she started to apologize for putting us all through this but I stopped her and reminded her she has nothing to apologize for. She is transitioning, it's a medical condition, she is accepted.

Victoria was of course, full steam ahead, champing at the bit to be put on female hormones that would begin to alter her outward appearance, and according to many of the transgendered women who posted about their own treatment online, bring a sense of calm. Whether that was a chemical effect of the hormones, or an emotional effect of finally receiving treatment and moving forward, we didn't know, but either way, calmer sounded good. I was still very anxious to slow down the process. The thought of Vicky being recognizably female to all and sundry horrified me. I had visions of our neighbours throwing bricks through the window, and being asked to leave the area or else. Walking about in Soho was one thing, popping into our local shops was quite another.

A much deeper fear was that, after everything we had been through, hormones would change Vicky's sexual orientation. We were up to this point, still lovers, except when we were shouting at each other obviously. What if after her treatment, she no longer wanted to be with me. What if she'd only been with me because she was male, and now she was female she wanted a man. The thought of going through all this only to be told that unfortunately she no longer felt able to be with a woman. That might actually be the dictionary definition of ironic. The painful truth was that if that were the outcome, she would still go ahead and that meant that though she loved me a lot, maybe it wouldn't be enough. Maybe she couldn't really love me?

Vicky found my continued desire to slow down the process incomprehensible. I kept saying I understood her condition and then asking her not to treat it. I tried to remind her that never mind the six months I'd had, what about her step-daughter? How much time was she going to be given to adjust to this? She tried to remind me she hadn't chosen to have this condition and what she needed was help and support not a brick wall at every turn. Maybe I didn't really love her? These were the things we quarrelled about. Still, we weren't screaming nearly as much.

It was still July. The shouting had mostly stopped, and we were managing to keep most of our discussions kind and respectful of each other. I posted online:

> One of the issues that is beginning to worry me quite a lot is the impact hormones may have on Vicky's personality. They are at the end of the day, just chemicals, they can't intelligently seek out the bits Vicky wants changing and leave alone the parts she likes. Vicky assures me that her personality won't change, but frankly, what does she know?
>
> I already know I have to remind Vicky when we're out shopping it's not all about her! I used to get taken out and looked after -- now I'm the one looking after her. Obviously we need to find a balance. The other evening as we were about to go out I said to her, 'you look lovely darling'. She smiled and looked very happy and then wandered off without a word about the effort I'd put into trying to look good. Small things I know, but still surprisingly hurtful, so I gently pointed out that I like being complimented too.
>
> I suppose the big worry is will I even recognize the person Vicky is to become. She is so determined to change everything about herself and willing to undergo whatever medical intervention that requires and, at the end of the day, even if that affected her sexual orientation and meant not wanting me anymore, the hard truth is, she wouldn't turn back.
>
> I'm just trying to take one day at a time, but it's hard knowing that 'forever' is now a negotiable part of our life together. Vicky of course, positive soul that she is, is convinced all will be well and I'm worrying about nothing.

The time had come, as far as Vicky was concerned, to tell the world and start living her life full time as the woman she really was. No more sneaking about leaving the house in long overcoats to conceal the dress beneath. This wasn't just selfish impatience on Vicky's behalf. The treatment she was seeking was absolutely reliant on her proving that she had lived 'in role', the doctors' words, not mine, as female for a whole year before they would give any drugs. So it wasn't that impatient to want to get going.

These words, these labels, are so powerful. They could inform so much and yet often they mislead. 'Living in role'. It's not fancy dress, it's not a game. This is living as your true self - what 'role' is there? The worst, most prevalent phrase though is 'Sex Change'. The medical term is Gender Corrective Surgery or GCS, or vaginoplasty, but the media seems very attached to the idea of the sex change operation. That so strongly implies that someone is born one gender and changes over to be the other gender. A man decides he might rather like to be a woman. A man who lost his genitals in a freak combine harvester accident, (bad example, work with me here) would still be a man. He would still know he was a man and you couldn't make him not a man no matter how much surgery you gave him. There's no such thing as a sex change. You are what you are. If you're born female, you're female, even if you're born with male genitals, you're female. Sorting out the physical results of too much testosterone at the wrong moment in the womb is not changing sex, it's just correcting a physical abnormality. So. No sex change, just corrective surgery. But I digress.

Vicky was determined that we would inform all of our neighbours, some of whom were great friends, others with whom we were simply on friendly smiling terms. They would all get the same letter. A 'Round Robin' to end all 'Round Robins'. Of course I wanted to wait, I always wanted to wait, but we worked on the letter together, trying to make sure it said what it needed to say and wasn't in any way aggressive or medically over-informative.

We had been invited as a family to an 18th birthday party for the daughter of close friends and of course there was no way Vicky could go. Her appearance even without hormones, was no longer 'normal' for a man. Her hair was too long, her eyebrows plucked and her ears pierced. We made an excuse of work or ill health or something and we went without her. I remember one of the guests asking me where that handsome husband of mine was. I lied like a professional and thought, 'where indeed'.

It was strange being at the party, not only without Vicky, but without anyone knowing that I was no longer the wife of Anthony. I had conversations about married life, plans for improving kitchens and possible holiday destinations. The life I was talking about no longer existed. It was all a lie and I was worryingly good at it. While I was at the party, Vicky was posting the letter through our neighbours' doors. I had asked her not to send it out tonight, but I knew she was going to anyway. She would face their immediate reactions alone. It was the fourth of July and Vicky was celebrating her independence. This is the letter.

Hello,

Please excuse the form of this letter. I am writing to all my friends and neighbours and it is not practical to write to each of you individually. I thought it would be easier to write you a letter as I have something to share. As you read on I am sure it will make more sense and you will agree its easier than if I had just come and knocked on you door to tell you.

I understand this may come as a surprise but I have recently been diagnosed with Gender Dysphoria. Essentially this means that though I appear male I am in fact female. I think it is fairer explaining these things to you in advance so that you understand that this is a medical condition and in no way poses a threat to you or your family. I have always valued the community that we have in our street and everyone's friendship. Your support and understanding would be even more welcome.

I hope you will continue reading and give me the chance to explain a little more fully.

I now understand this to be a medical condition that has been with me since childhood. It is not a psychiatric delusion and it is not going to go away - I have to address it.

Many people call it Gender Identity Dysphoria or GID. It is a condition recognised by the NHS as developed pre-natally and it means that I self identify as female and have done from a very early age, therefore I find living as a man intensely distressing. If you think of it as being a woman who's constantly being 'mistaken' for a man because of a severe hormone imbalance then hopefully it makes more sense.

My physical body is male but my physical brain is female. The brain cannot be altered but the body can. I have now reached the stage where I need to notify you of my intention to align my gender and as part of that process I am beginning to present to the outside world as female and I will be changing my name legally to Victoria.

I haven't begun any physical changes yet and I'm aware I don't pass as female, so it will initially be counterintuitive for people to use female pronouns. However the NHS requires that I live in the female role before hormone therapy can begin and though this means initially I may appear like a man in female clothing as the hormones take their effect this will hopefully diminish.

One of the things I have learnt about myself is that whatever I look like on the outside, the inner me has always been the same person and will pretty much stay that way even after changing the outside appearance.

I understand that you may have questions, please feel free to ask Emma or myself and if not face-to-face then you can always email me or just drop a note through the door.

But please also understand that this is a very challenging time for us as a family and what would be appreciated more than anything is your support and compassion.

If you don't feel able to give that, though we will be sad we will understand and hope that at least you can respect our rights and we will do our best to respect yours.

If you would like to research more about this yourself then may I suggest http://www.gires.org.uk

Thank you for taking the time to read this

By the time I got home everyone at our end of the street knew all about Vicky. Their reaction had been uniformly positive. One lovely person came rushing over to give Vicky a hug, others sent a card of congratulation. I was rather sorry to have missed it. No-one withdrew their friendship, no-one threw bricks. Vicky was very happy and I was very relieved. I hadn't seen any of our neighbours yet and I did feel pretty uncomfortable that all my secret life was now out and available for discussion. People who wouldn't dream of asking personal questions directly of Vicky had no such trouble with me and over the next few days I found myself with inquiries about how her genitalia would be altered and how our sex life would function. One well meaning friend speculated that we must now, surely, live 'as sisters'. Another suggested that loss of a sex life was probably a small price to pay for a secure home. I didn't contradict them, because really it wasn't anyone's business.

Quite a few married couples told us that our news had caused some very deep discussions between themselves about how they would deal with such a situation. The most usual conclusion was they just couldn't imagine it but hoped they would be able to stay together. Some felt sure it was not something they could accept, but that I was very wonderful for trying. It was nice to hear that so many people thought staying together was a positive outcome, even if not all of them thought we'd succeed. In a way it made me feel more normal. We were a nice couple, and people still wanted to know us.

The experience is not the same for all transgendered people. Some of them do just cut all ties and move cities in order to start afresh with no one to explain to or wait for. It can be a lonely choice. Others try to bring friends and family along but are met with prejudice and rejection. They too can find themselves facing the hardest moments of their life alone. Some move on with never a backward glance and others are so traumatized they never look forward. Having said all that, many have found success happiness and love, and all as themselves. Not all of them feel the need to inform those around them of their medical history. Many tell no one, which is called being 'in stealth'.

Many debates on transgender supports sites focus on the rights and wrongs of such a decision. Part of the argument says 'Why should I tell anyone my private medical history, it's no one's business but my own'. Another part says, if the only transgendered people visible are those in the early stages of transition, who look like blokes in frocks, then that's what we will be seen as. What hope have we of being understood by society. The last, most disturbing aspect of the argument points to the murder rates of transgendered people against the rest of the population. It's not good. In 2010 over a thousand transgendered people across the world were murdered.

If hate comes from fear, then it's fear we have to tackle to help people see the most important word in the phrase 'transgendered person', is 'person'.

Vicky had sent out her letter to many of her oldest friends. As Anthony she had been part of a very close group. They had done everything together since their teens. They went on ski trips, hung out in pubs, played computer games. Two of them had known Anthony since childhood and were as close as brothers. Their acceptance mattered very much to Vicky. It wasn't to be an instant result. Initially the responses ranged from disbelief to actual anger. One friend declared that Anthony was clearly mad and wanted nothing more to do with him. Vicky's oldest and closest friend was clearly finding this news challenging. He had been best man at our wedding and was very clear that whatever his friend might feel, he was a he. Why had Anthony married me if he felt like this. This was a selfish and un-choosable choice. Get help and sort yourself out seemed to be the message. One email was so unkind that I felt the need to send my own reply. Particularly to challenge the idea that Vicky had made a selfish choice. There was no choice in being transgendered. What kind of insane masochist would choose to go through this?, I asked. We were doing this because we had to, this was the only way forward.

Despite occasional flare-ups, we were beginning to try to function like a regular family again. The normality was healing. To be able to think about something other than transition was bliss.

Wed Jul 08, 2009 7:05 pm

All the support and advice we have received has got us to this point. I can't quite believe it. All our family and nearly all our friends now know about Vicky, and as I type this Vicky is in the kitchen, wearing a lovely silk Kaftan top with black linen trousers and the silver heart locket I bought her, cooking supper. Normal quiet evening. Our Ellie is on a sleepover, but if she had come home, none of this would have needed to change. As Vicky says, wow wow wow.

That mention of Vicky's outfit makes me smile. Like many trans women who transition a little later in life, Vicky had missed out on living as a woman for her teens, her twenties and her thirties. Her dress sense, on the whole was pretty catastrophic. Denied the opportunity of three decades of practice, she had no idea how, or much desire, to dress appropriately for a 39 year old woman. Why, I used to ask, do they all want to wear mini-skirts?! What's with the sparkly stockings and the tight revealing tops?? Do you see any other women in their late thirties wandering around in Barbie-pink leggings??? Poor love, She was trying to make up for lost time. Learning, but also experiencing each missed decade one after another. Eventually we got to stylish, but we had our share of moments when Vicky presented herself ready to go out and I just said 'No'. It was like having another daughter to guide through the mysteries of womanhood.

Make-up was also a steep learning curve. This was more tricky, Vicky's dark hispanic colouring was so different from my own pale northern european face. I didn't really know what was going to work. Also, I did not have stubble to contend with. Vicky had bought make-up to cover the worst of it, but it needed to be applied with a trowel to have any effect, and we all know once trowels are involved, you've probably gone too far. Generally though, it was just a question of gently putting the brakes on. It wasn't just which make-up she chose. It was the amount of time she required to put it on. I remember being a teenager and spending entire evenings applying make-up, tirelessly retouching and perfecting every aspect until it was time for bed and I had to take it all off again. I understand that's what was going on with Vicky, but after nigh on forty years of applying make-up I had got it down to 30 seconds. Having to wait an additional hour and a half for Vicky to do essentially the same thing, drove me nuts, and when she did finally come down I usually ended up saying, 'your eyes look really lovely but you're not going out in that skirt!'. That may sound very controlling on my part, but I was trying to get us stared at less and Vicky's style decisions could be quite attention grabbing.

A month after Ellie's birthday I decided that she and I should go away on holiday together, without Vicky. We all needed some time to process life and to take the pressure off. I wanted to do something fun with Ellie, so in a moment of madness we booked a package holiday to Benalmadena, on the spanish Costa del Sol. I am more of a self catering, tromping across the moors kind of gal and Benalmadena was a bit of a culture shock. Sun sea and el Mini Disco. We both giggled our way through restaurants determined to serve us egg and chips and family entertainments that we watched with increasing bemusement.

There was one surreal evening when two tour guides tried to get the children dancing to a selection of 80's pop whilst dressed as a nun and a gangster. The gangster had a plastic machine gun which he held against the nun's head as he pretended to riddle her with a stream of bullets. What fun. Everyone else laughed and cheered. Maybe this was the annual holiday of the humanist society. We were speechless.

We spent our days on the beach reading and searching for the mythic spanish seafood restaurant. On the third day we found it. Not a Sunday lunch on offer and a menu with food from the sea, cooked by spanish people using spanish recipes. It was just like Putney. In the evenings we hid in our room, terrified the tour guides would make us join in with one of their merry entertainments. We watched some very bizarre american television. The working life of a beach policeman in Florida is a subject about which we are both now surprisingly well informed.

We didn't talk about Vicky until the very end of the holiday. Ellie was so protective of me, but it felt like everything was upside down. I was meant to be looking after her, guiding her through this emotional maze, and all I could do was keep apologizing to her and saying helplessly, 'I just don't know what to do'. She would comfort me and tell me it was fine, she was not going to be scarred for life and if Vicky could just lay off the heavy handed parenting, that would be fine too. On the last night the movie on offer was 'Kinky Boots', the true story of a Midlands shoe manufacturer who saved his business by catering to the niche market of Transvestites and drag-queens. Ellie and I watched it knowing we knew more about this subject than we had expected, but we still cheered at the end when the shoe manufacturer realized drag queens are people too.

We went home. Vicky met us at the airport and we both hugged her. Life went on. It was the middle of July and my mother was celebrating her 83rd birthday. I knew that my younger sister who lived in Canterbury had been kept up to date with all our dramas by my mother so I was hopeful when I phoned her. Her initial reaction had been, 'that's fine, no worries, I suspected something was up'. She had asked if she and her partner could join us for a pub lunch to celebrate our mum's 83rd birthday. I mentioned, just to be clear, that Vicky was now living in the female role full time and so it would be Vicky and me who would be turning up to the pub. No more 'Anthony'.

That, it seemed , changed things, though she didn't tell me that at the time. I found out when I asked my mother what time they would be arriving at which point she had to say 'they're not coming'. My sister didn't feel she could 'cope' so to speak. I think the truth was she was worried she would laugh to see her brother in law in a dress and lipstick. I can understand that reaction, it's a very

71

basic human instinct to express discomfort at anything different by laughing. It's a fear response, the same as chimpanzees pulling back there lips to show they're anxious. I get it. I just hoped my sister would be able to get beyond that one day. I knew my mother was really hurt. I was really hurt. It made me uncomfortable when other people responded like that. It cut away my confidence that we would ever be able to live as just another couple. My sister did get her head around it in the end and we are still on her invitation list for her mad birthday teas, a combination of huge amounts of food and the most fiendish games of 'Pass the Parcel' known to man.

But despite the people who seemed to be backing away, there were two who took me by surprise with their open hearts. We went to have tea with the family of Vicky's four year old Godchild. Even driving there I was anxious about how they would respond to meeting Vicky. She had changed a lot since they last saw her. Acceptance by email or phone may not be the same when confronted by the reality of your lately male friend still visible beneath the makeup. But I needn't have worried, they were so lovely to us both, and encouraged the children to play with Vicky. By the end of the day, both children were asking if Aunty Vicky could stay and if not when was she coming back? It was wonderful for both of us to feel so accepted. They both expressed the belief that Vicky made much more sense than Anthony. This made all the bits that didn't fit fall into place. When people treated us like this I was able to relax. Who Vicky was, who we were, was acceptable, unusual but not wrong, just different.

They also raised a very difficult subject for us. Church. Vicky had been raised Catholic and I, though raised atheist, had been Christian since my teens and Catholic since my twenties. My children had made their holy communion in my local church, I had sung in the choir and been a regular face at mass. The Catholic church does not acknowledge the existence of transgendered people. They are, according to the church, sinful in their desire to mess with their God-given gender. According to the present Pope, there are only two genders and God doesn't make mistakes. A transgendered person would be treated sympathetically within a parish, but on the firm understanding they were, as one rather intense young priest told us, an abomination unto the lord. Oh dear.

If neither of us had any faith this would be of little importance. Walk away and never look back. We thought about brazening it out and taking our place in the parish, but the question was then, why were we supporting an institution that denied our existence. I know several gay and transgendered people who do manage to square the circle, saying that it's our church, we just disagree with that particular teaching. It's wrong, simple as that. I didn't feel comfortable with that. I don't have any doubt God loves Vicky, he made her after all, she is not an abomination unto the Lord or anyone else. Attending mass seemed to me to sign up to all the Catholic church's teaching, and I just couldn't. Its standpoint also allowed others to justify their own bigotry by pointing to Her teaching. It was a lasting sadness that I feel cut off from the Catholic church because it didn't keep up to date with medical knowledge. Or maybe I've misunderstood. Anyway, God is Love - extrapolate. We did eventually find a welcome in our local Anglican church which is determinedly inclusive and the richer for it.

Vicky's relationship with her step-daughter continued to be a source of tension and unhappiness. Vicky so needed everything to be resolved. She obsessively analyzed every interaction, every conversation, such as they were, and found them wanting. By now, she felt, Ellie should have got over any surprise or shock, have understood Vicky's truth, repaired any temporary damage to their relationship and moved on. Poor Ellie was still very unsure of who this person was. Were they the same underneath or had something deeper changed. She still felt quite angry and let down. Vicky was utterly unable to see any of that as reasonable or even to be expected. It made her very unhappy and angry. I could understand the difficulties Vicky was having, and why she was having them, but I could also see Ellie was doing her best, and to expect more was unrealistic and unkind. I was in the middle trying to keep a fragile peace intact, between a rock and a hard place. I vented my growing frustration online.

Thurs Jul 30, 2009 12:01 pm

The Rock being Vicky and the hard place being my Ellie and me being the idiot in the middle. Arggghhhh. I just can't seem to get Vicky to stop feeling let down by Ellie's failure to engage in discussion. She's 16 for goodness sake - she struggles to talk about any feelings, why should this be any different???? She's been away for the last week with her aunty in France and she's away for another week but after that we are all going to have to live in the same space without biting each other's heads off.

I just don't seem able to get through to Vicky that by insisting on her 'rights' as parent she risks loosing everything with her step-daughter. Vicky says I don't need to be in the middle here, but honestly where else can I be? I'm not going to tell Ellie to stop being difficult about this because it upsets Vicky.. I'm not going to tell Vicky to stop her journey because Ellie finds it challenging! All I can do is ask both of them to think about how the other must be feeling.

So here I sit, stuck in the middle wanting the happiness of both of them and if it's not too much to ask... Me

How had I ended up here again? Focusing all my energy on trying to ensure other people's happiness and forgetting about my own.

Ah, self-pity is a wonderful thing. You can be miserable and enjoy yourself at the same time. What an idiot. The trouble was I really did want them both to be happy, and I believed if I could achieve that, then I would be happy. Things started getting very shouty again. Conversations quickly lost their balance and they were always, always about Ellie. Our relationship, Vicky's and mine, seemed to have got lost in this overwhelming need to have Ellie's full acceptance. I felt so disappointed, because I had really believed we were through the worst and things were going to go in a nice straight line getting better and better. As I said, what an idiot. I tried to make sense of it all and look to myself for some of the problem.

I certainly wasn't ever willing to let Vicky and Ellie sort it out without me. I always needed to intervene and protect. The arguments between them triggered such a feeling of fear in me. I didn't want my child to be shouted at, but it was more than that. I felt a horrible sense of having been here before. Memories of my childhood all being dragged out of the depths to cause trouble in my consciousness. It felt destabilizing to have these painful thoughts interfere with the process of each day. I wanted, I needed to be the reasonable one in the middle, understanding both points of view and gently guiding. Instead I was bringing my own selection of unexamined anxieties to the mix. Honestly, if you'd had us all holding lit fireworks it couldn't have been more explosive. Something had to give.

One evening after yet another day of hurt and anger we had yet another very intense conversation - we both lost it - but something really important and to me deeply unexpected came out of it. I had not realized how real to me was my fear of the children being hurt. Vicky had been trying to go step by step with Ellie yet I kept telling her she was doing it all wrong, and I couldn't come up with any example.why was I so afraid - and I mean so stomach churningly all out panic afraid?

I had loaded not only my fear about how the children would cope with Vicky's transition, but the fear from every previous situation, right back to the lack of protection I felt in the face of my father's mental illness and his violence towards me and my siblings. Even my 'failure' to protect my son from autism (I know that one wasn't my fault but when did that ever stop a mother feeling guilty?). I needed to start responding to what was happening right now, rather than everything that had ever happened. It was way too much baggage to bring to such a difficult situation.

Transition is not just the experience of the transgendered person. It is the whole family, coming to terms with their own new position not only with each other, but in society. Mother not of a son, but a daughter, no longer a wife but partner to a woman, step-daughter to a woman not a man. I had my own transition to make.

The issue of Vicky's title within the family was surprisingly tricky. She very much wanted to be recognised as a step-mother. I wasn't having that. Ellie had a mother, she had no need of a second one. Vicky was going to have to accept being referred to as step-parent, and not because I thought so. This was Ellie's decision. It wasn't about what Vicky wanted or needed and it wasn't about me either.

In retrospect it's amazing that I still thought it was Vicky and Vicky alone who needed counselling. We had so many complicated areas to deal with. So many assumptions to reshape, as individuals and as a family. Really I had just as much need to start talking and unravelling as she did, but at this stage I was too busy seeing Vicky as the problem to be solved and the rest of us as the 'normal' people around her. It's quite a common solution within a family, I am told, to designate one person as the problem, allowing the rest of the family to dump all bad stuff at their door. Common but wrong. As Vicky became more and more distressed over her situation, the possibility of resolving it within the normal structure of a family became smaller and smaller. And now the time had come to tell my son.

It was the beginning of August, the day after my birthday and I went to visit him on my own. This time even Vicky could see that was the best idea. There was no way of telling how he would react and I had long experience of how to talk to my lad. He listened very intently as I explained the medical realities, the practical difficulties and what I was planning to do about them. Then I told him it was absolutely his choice how much or how little contact he wanted to have with Vicky or with me. He said, 'The only perfect person died on a cross two thousand years ago. We're all monsters, just trying to find the beauty within the beast'. It was the most poetic and beautiful response I had had. I felt so proud of him. He was understanding this a hundred times better than me and so quickly. It seemed the dream response and I congratulated myself I must have handled the whole thing very well. Also, I must have raised him very well to instill such an open heart despite all his problems. I congratulated myself quite a lot.

My boy is complicated. Second-guess him at your peril. He has always been a very thoughtful person, but sometimes things take a bit of time to process, and the first reaction may not be the lasting one. I was so delighted by his response that I forgot it might not last. A few days later I asked him if he'd thought anymore about Vicky's news. He said he didn't want to talk about 'that person'. In fact, he didn't want to have anything to with her. He understood perfectly well that she was a transgendered woman, but he felt lied to and tricked into accepting a step-father who didn't exist. There was no discussion to be had, that's how he felt. A few days after that he called home for a chat. He wanted me of course, but Vicky happened to pick up the phone. He politely asked to talk to me and that was that. Then a few days after that, he called again. He needed to know something about guitars. Something I certainly didn't know about, so grudgingly he agreed to talk to Vicky about it. Within seconds he was chatting away, all reserve forgotten. He said he would call her Vic, because it was more androgynous, and if she came to visit, it should be in trousers. Vicky was happy to accept such small compromises to have this level of normality with him.

That was the reaction that stuck. He said it wasn't so hard for him because he didn't live with us, but he was happy to walk around his home town with us, go into restaurants and cinemas and never expressed any embarrassment. Caused a bit though. A few weeks later we were all walking through a trendy part of town, known for it's diverse population and cool shops. There was a poster advertising a 'Women only sex shop'. 'There you are,' he said loudly, 'You can both go there, it's for lesbians'.

Chapter Five

Vicky was now the proud owner of a UK passport, that stated her gender as female. A change of name deed document witnessed by the solicitor, and a letter from the GP confirming she was living full time and undergoing treatment, had been all that was needed. When Vicky went to pick up the passport, she was asked 'are you collecting this for someone else?'. When she said, 'no' the lady went and got her supervisor, who checked the documentation and gave Vicky her passport without any more questions.

I was very glad it was sorted out. I had worried how she could possibly travel abroad, looking as she did but with a passport that said 'Male' and belonged to Anthony. The photograph was all but unrecognizable. Now the name and photo matched the reality. It was one small ray of light in an increasingly stormy sky. Everything at home seemed to be falling to pieces. Despite my earlier optimism, we were not moving swiftly towards happy ever after. In the middle of August Vicky went to America on a photographic project. I was actually relieved at the prospect of some time without her.

Her relationship with Ellie was strained. Although Ellie was trying to take this huge alteration in her stride, it was not enough for Vicky who still didn't seem able to offer patience in the face of fairly standard teenage behaviour. In Vicky's eyes, her step-daughter was not moving forward fast enough, and she resented it terribly. At the same time it was all I could do to stop Ellie giving up in the face of so little understanding. When Vicky left for America, Ellie gave her a goodbye hug. It was really affectionate full arms hug and, I was sure Vicky would be overjoyed. Her response was an irritated 'Where's my smile - can't you manage a smile?'. There was so little comprehension of what it must have cost Ellie to give her that hug, to give an act of loving acceptance which drew a line under the father daughter relationship and instead accepted the new relationship and reached out to it. Vicky was only annoyed by such an act. I could have throttled her.

This, far more than any gender issue, was what would do for us. I drove Vicky to the airport. An hour long journey during which she shouted at me about how unfair it was and how I favoured Ellie over her. I did my best to keep quiet with the occasional 'I can see you're hurting'. This was not because I was full of saintly compassion, simply that I knew what would happen if I started venting how I actually felt. It was not much fun. Vicky was now so enveloped in pain she really couldn't see beyond it. The focus for this pain had become the 'lost' relationship with her step-daughter, a magnet for all the despair and fear inside her. I wish I had understood that better at the time, because all I could see was an unreasonable focus on my child as though she were withholding the keys to Vicky's happiness.

Add to this that Ellie had just turned 16, a tricky time in anyone's life without their dad becoming a second mum. It was very hard to unravel what was related to our unique situation and what was just life with a 16 year old. One day, While Vicky was still abroad, Ellie spoke to me about the loss of her step-dad. She could still see him in Vicky, and she missed him. It was a brave thing to admit to.

Why couldn't I get this through to Vicky? How many times would I have to tell her to be patient? How many times could she ignore her therapist, my mother, her friends with kids - all saying how lucky she was to have a step-daughter willing to try to understand. She just couldn't see it. How long can one bang one's head against a brick wall before getting knocked out? Not this long, I thought.

Before she went to the States, I had finally agreed to go to a counselling session with Vicky. I think I had been very much seeing Vicky as the problem, the one who needed fixing, but we both had our issues and I needed help just as much. The office was in central London on the third floor of a very smart block of flats. The little lift was just big enough for two people, or three very friendly people. The waiting room was carpeted and furnished with comfortable leather armchairs. On the coffee table were magazines. The titles were not one's I'd come across before. 'Transliving', with a glossy front cover showed a glamorous woman with long brown curly hair and very made-up face, all slightly soft-focus and a bit too much cleavage. It was somewhere between Woman's weekly and FHM. The articles were very much focussed on where to find heels that fit and which false breasts would give the most natural look.

On the shelf in the corner were a series of pastel church candles in varying sizes. They were attached to the shelf with small chains. This seemed excessively protective for candles, until I realized they weren't candles. They were dilators - a dildo shaped object designed to help a post-operative transexual increase and stabalize the size of her vagina. At this stage of the game that was a bit too much information as far as I was concerned.

The counselling itself was a very useful experience. The counsellor was neither judgmental or so opinion-less that there was nothing to lean against. I listened to Vicky express her pain at Ellie's 'failures' to get with the programme. She was so desperate not to ruin everything with Ellie, that she was ruining everything with Ellie. And she could not see it. That seemed to be at the root of the shouting, and we hadn't even started hormones yet. She very much saw everyone's advice as 'ganging up' on her. Like any creature trapped in a corner, she lashed out. I felt so angry, I really didn't have anything sensible to offer. The counsellor gently untangled thoughts and feelings and challenged Vicky and me to think about it in a different way. This was hugely constructive. This was a way to hear and to be heard. There was so much built up hurt and resentment on both sides which was going to have to come out. Better in the safety of a counselling session than all over the kitchen table. It wasn't going to be a one session solution, but it might actually work.

A few days after she had gone to America, I sent Vicky an email reminding her of the kind gentle thoughtful person she had always been. That was who Ellie needed as a parent. I understood, I told her, that all this rage and stress was a passing phase, but for Ellie's sake, and for hers and mine too, we had to get beyond that. Vicky's transition and it's impact had become the sole topic of conversation between us. It dominated every minute of every day. I knew that was unsustainable, but I didn't know how to stop. She came home from her trip and we picked up the last argument where we had left off.

The worst was yet to come. In September, nine months after Vicky had first realized she had to transition, nine months of both of us trying so very hard to hold it together, Vicky had her second breakdown. It was as though the anger of one argument rolled into the next until there was nothing left but shouting and anger. She was unlivable with. I couldn't do it anymore and I wouldn't expose Ellie to it anymore either. I had thought we were ripping the wallpaper off, but the truth was the whole building was falling down. Trying to stay together as though nothing was happening was impossible. I knew if we did this to our relationship any longer, there wouldn't be any relationship to save. No, that's not true, I wasn't thinking a month, or even a week ahead. At that moment I just wanted the shouting to stop. I couldn't live under that level of stress and Vicky couldn't see what the problem was, all she saw was how unreasonable I was and how unsupportive . Though I did my share of shouting and, I'm sure, unfair statements, I still think Vicky wins the all-over gold medal. She told me, as yet another argument drew to it's weary conclusion, 'You've changed'. Pot, Kettle, black.

I went to my sisters with Ellie and I asked Vicky to move out. She could go and live with her mother. It was our lowest moment and though it solved the immediate problem it caused a whole other set that I didn't foresee. Once you start allowing other people to pass judgement on the state of your relationship, you also give them certain rights to advise on what to do next. If you don't follow that advice, they will be more than a little disappointed. Hindsight eh. Marvelous.

How had we come to this. I knew we loved each other, really loved each other and yet we were separated, like a couple who had had enough of each other and were preparing to make the final break of divorce. Except I didn't want a divorce. I didn't want this alternative future without Vicky. Yes of course if I could have waved a magic wand and had Anthony, non-transgendered, like all the other blokes I knew, then I would have waved it. I think Vicky would have too. I knew that was a fantasy, and I wasn't holding out for it. I had been so determined that I was kind enough, bright enough, wonderful enough to drag us all through this awful time and come out the other end together, a family. Why wasn't it happening like that? Didn't true love mean happy ever after.

The day Vicky moved into her mother's was the day she took her first hormones. After months of psychiatric assessments she had finally be judged to be, as we both knew perfectly well, a transgendered woman in need of treatment. Because Vicky's body will never be able to produce the female hormones they should have, she will always have to take medication to replace them. They come in various forms, Vicky started on pills - one a day. It must have been a euphoric moment, but I was not there to share it with her. I was watching determination in action from a distance. Even though we had separated and everything seemed so disastrous, she was ploughing on with her treatment. I felt very low down the list of what was important to her. If she really loved me, she wouldn't take those bloody hormones, I thought.

Vicky and I weren't speaking, texting, anything. It was a strange calm. Life at home became very peaceful, it was like being back in the maisonette, just Ellie and me, no arguments no shouting. That time did us good, we needed peace, but I can't begin to imagine what Vicky was going through. She did not think we were having a break to calm down, she thought it was all over. As I wasn't talking to her there was no way to put her right. If she wanted to collect anything from our home, I insisted she phone first to make sure we would be out. She was facing her transition on her own and it seemed to be following the well trodden path of rejection and loneliness so often documented online. She couldn't turn back though. Even if she really loved me, she couldn't turn back. If I couldn't love her like this then she just had to lose me.

A few days later a hand written letter dropped through the letter-box. It was delivered not by Vicky, but by a friend acting as go-between. I suppose I had been very firm on the subject of leaving me alone and not coming anywhere near the house when I was there. The letter showed how very sad she was. Vicky said if I did indeed accept her and want to be with her, then our problems were other things and we needed to sort them out. If her behaviour was destroying our family then she wanted to understand it and change it. Would I come to couple's counselling? She was already seeing her specialist transgender counsellor once a week and she wanted me to start coming with her to that on a regular basis. She also wanted us to try good old-fashioned marriage counselling where we might be able to rebuild our relationship, even though we were still living apart. We would meet twice a week and go to counselling then she would drop me home and go away. It felt like a step forward. I sent her a text. 'Yes'.

We had problems, but they were not insurmountable and we still loved each other. We were both, it seemed, endlessly hopeful. Maybe with couples counselling we would not build up unsaid unhappiness until it exploded in that all to familiar destructive way. The problem, for me at least, was no longer the fact of her gender. It is all to easy to think that this huge challenge must have been the root of all unhappiness, but it wasn't. We were just a couple with the same baggage and fears as a middle of the road heterosexual couple. I had been shocked and challenged and frightened. All sorts of things, but I'd got over it. It was not her gender, it was her anger. Her transexualism had opened the floodgates to a lifetime of emotional hurts, they were what was hurting me. I wanted to work it out. I wanted us to get back to happy.

I still believed that at the end of all this there might be a happy ending. The sheer pain of being apart though, was all but unbearable. Again I cried so much my eyes swelled shut. Days and days. My mother and my sister were very worried for me, there was just no containing the distress. They wanted to tell me it would be alright, they would all be there for me, help me make a new life. I had been wonderful for trying to stay, but it really was an impossibility and I should move on with my life. The thought of a future without Vicky was beyond my imagining. I tried to visualize it and I couldn't. I tried to see how we could possibly go back to the screaming and shouting, and I couldn't. The path had crumbled into an abyss in front of me and there was no way forward and no way back, so I cried.

Finally my mother, who was beginning to worry for my sanity, came up with a solution. We would separate in the short term, in order to stay together in the long term. I needed to raise Ellie without all this trauma. Vicky needed to focus on her journey without the emotional and financial burden of trying to be a parent and a partner. I understood that many trans women go a bit haywire during transition, but by the time the storm was over the damage was done and the relationship gone. The moment she told me I thought 'I can accept this and if Vicky can too then it's not over'. I stepped back from the abyss, there was a way to have a future with Vicky. Just not yet.

So we would separate. Sell our house, both rent somewhere for the next two years. Vicky would make her journey without having to worry about hurting anyone. We would be at a safe distance. Once Ellie had gone to university, we would come together again and ask ourselves the simple question - 'is this who I want to spend the rest of my life with?' I believed it would be, and that thought, finally, enabled me to stop crying. It was a good thing, I looked like a Cabbage Patch doll.

I think my family hoped that this 'plan' would soften the blow of ending our relationship. I obviously couldn't cope with it in one fell swoop, so they would help me break it to myself gently. Maybe, I don't know if they actually thought this, I would meet someone else in the meantime and be able to put this very sad time of my life behind me. Anyway, whatever their thinking, they did not like it when I received texts from Vicky. They had watched me brought to the very edge and they saw Vicky as the author of all that. It's understandable they wanted me to find the strength to walk away.

The plan had taken the terror out of being apart. It felt more like when she had been abroad. We would have late night phone calls and send long emails to each other. Sometimes I could even imagine it was Anthony I was talking to on the phone. It was still his voice. I didn't tell my family about those calls and emails, but I think they were on to me. We went to see the estate-agent together and explained we needed to sell the house and get a little flat for Ellie and me - Vicky would continue living at her mum's - and then later we would buy a house together.

It was certainly easier after the months of such intensity to communicate with none of the pressures of daily life to distract us. No shouting and no arguing. We treasured the time we had together, because we knew it would be brief. It was as though we'd gone back to dating. We didn't waste our time with all the serious realities.

Vicky would come to the house in the daytime, while Ellie was at school, but go before she got back. Maybe this is what having an affair feels like, I can understand why people get swept up in the thrill of the secret. Though in our case it was a badly kept secret. My family felt I was not sticking to the bargain. The idea was that we should not see each other for at least two years and ideally not communicate in any way. Cold Turkey. Otherwise how would I move on? Moving on was not my idea of happy ever after.

I was facing a particularly unique challenge that needed a particularly unique solution. I knew it looked as though I was jumping ship, I know Vicky was worried that was what I was doing, but truly, I was not. I honestly believed this was the course of action that would lead to Vicky and me spending the rest of our lives together. Trying to stay together as though nothing was happening had actually made things worse. Vicky needed space to be however she needed to be to get through this. Sometimes, if you need to bring all the plaster off the ceiling, it's not a very good idea to stand underneath it. Sometimes you might need to stand outside for a bit. It made sense. At last we were doing something positive to secure our long term future.

Of course I wished we could achieve all this with Vicky in situ, Selling the house and renting a flat. All that disruption was daunting, but at the end of the day, it was just stuff, and stuff is never more important than people. If this was the price to keep Vicky it was worth paying. Things had got very very bad, now they were getting better. All those months ago I prayed for guidance and heard the words 'love is the answer'. We both still believed that.

I was a single parent again. Ellie was still too angry and upset with Vicky to even talk about her, let alone with her. It was very hard to see her distress. She had lost her step-dad, and now we were getting ready to move again.

A week later I got a call from my son's college to say he'd gone missing. Someone had foolishly believed him when he claimed to know his way back from town. He hadn't been seen for two hours. All I could think about was his cavalier attitude to crossing roads and his gentle heart that would go wherever he was told. What if someone got hold of him. I was so afraid and there was absolutely nothing I could do but wait. Finally there was a call. Clever lad, he'd gone to the college, the one place he knew how to get to. It was closed for the holidays so he sat on a boulder in the car park. Thankfully a member of staff searching for him checked the college. He was sitting there, in the dark. Thank God. All evidence that he wasn't ready to live independently just yet. An argument I had to make on my own at his next review. No Vicky to hold my hand. To tell me not to panic. To hug me when it was all alright. I missed her for so many reasons, and everything that happened seemed to underline how much.

The 17th of September, 2009 was Vicky's 40th birthday. We had, years ago, planned that it would be a big party with all our friends. Turning forty was a big deal, it was also Vicky's first birthday as herself. There should have been a party. There couldn't be, of course, because everything was in such a mess. Instead Vicky and I, much to the disapproval of my family, met up in Richmond Park for a picnic. We met in the car park like two cold war spies. It was a little surreal sitting in glorious isolation, occasionally passed by dogs and their owners wrapped up against the cold, but I had brought hot tea and chicken and pudding. It was a great picnic. And we both felt very happy. Whatever else, we were at least together for her birthday.

I had bought Vicky a necklace and matching earrings, they were red and heart shaped. Vicky was thrilled and touched that I should buy her such a gift. It was a present for a woman who was loved.

After the picnic we strolled about for a while. In the isolation I was happy to hold her hand. We sat down on an old tree stump and embraced. Just to feel those arms around me, to feel that cheek pressed against mine, felt so right and so natural. Everything we had been through seemed so incredibly unimportant next to this truth. We loved each other. This was what we had been fighting for. This was why we were going through all this hell. This love, this closeness was worth having. Back at the car park we got into our separate cars and drove away, and that just felt wrong.

My family were very concerned that I was slipping back into bad habits, like Toad in the smoking room, having promised to be separate from Vicky for at least two years, I was in daily contact with her and now had met up with her, not for counselling, which was OK, but for her birthday, which was not. What about my children they wanted to know. How could this possibly be good for them. I had to be strong, not think of my own selfish desires but about what was best for them. There are few mother's who would respond well to being told they didn't know what was best for their children and I was not one of them. Suddenly my tight knit support network felt more like a cage.

I do understand why my family were so worried. They had witnessed the breakdown of our wonderful happy life and Vicky had, undoubtedly, said and done some pretty extreme things, but then she was in a pretty extreme situation. We were trying to get beyond that, and that meant understanding and forgiving. I wasn't about to force Ellie to 'forgive' Vicky if she wasn't ready, but honestly I think she understood better than anyone else, what had driven that behaviour and that Vicky was trying to do better. My family wanted things to be wonderful for my children and me. That's not an unreasonable thing to want. Surely this strange man who had turned out to be a woman, and then screamed at everyone for several months, couldn't be the way forward? The trouble was, for them my moving on and not being with Vicky anymore was a possible outcome, and for me it wasn't.

I say Vicky was trying to do better, but it was by no means an instant success. And all the while she was racing forward as fast as she could with her transition. She had discovered from several of the other transgendered women online, that there was a doctor in Thailand who specialized in GCS and would be willing to operate with proof of one, not two years of 'living in role', and the necessary psychiatric sign-offs. Her attitude was still the sooner the better, and yes, I expect if my vagina looked like a penis I'd want the damn thing dealt with as soon as possible. I did understand, but we were still in such a fragile state as a family, by no means stable enough to cope with surgery abroad, and not just abroad, but the other side of the world. Where was I supposed to be during all this? By Vicky's side? By Ellie's side? Being only one of me, I could see a problem. Again I found myself saying to Vicky, 'For God's sake, slow down, think of the impact on us, not yet'.

The counselling was at least moving us forward, tiny step by tiny step. We were talking about so much more than the fact that one of us was transgendered.

it was forcing Vicky to face a lot of painful stuff. It became obvious why she had waited so long before exploring her gender issues. Her father, fighting his own demons, was in no position to be supportive about a condition even less understood twenty years ago than it is now. Vicky had sought some control over her own life in her twenties by becoming anorexic. Then she had turned to alcohol, drugs, anything to blot out that unlivable truth, 'I am female'. There was a lot of past hurt to deal with. Sometimes I felt frustrated that breakthroughs made in counselling seemed to evaporate as soon as we got outside the door. She would seem to understand in the session, but ten minutes later would be saying 'but WHY won't Ellie talk to me?'. Patience was not in her vocabulary.

The discussions regarding her GCS in Thailand continued through November, One day the counsellor said to Vicky 'you are very in touch with how you feel about everything but you don't show any awareness that Emma or Ellie might have feelings'. I don't think she was able to take it on board, but at least someone other than me had said it, without suggesting that meant I should dump her. The idea of waiting for corrective surgery because someone else isn't ready for it, is very challenging. To this day Vicky and I don't quite agree on the rights and wrongs of it. the truth is, I think, that of course everyone's body is their own and they must do what they need to do, but there will be consequences if you can't give those around you time to catch up. It isn't a question of whether or not a partner 'should' stay, it's a question of whether they will. It's not a question of a person's 'right' to have their surgery, it's whether they can cope with the impact on their relationships. Each individual person has to weigh that up and decide.

I had trusted the fact that being attracted to Vicky and able to love her for herself would be enough, but it was, it seemed, the least of our challenges. The real Vicky, the one who had gone missing in action just at the moment, would have been very concerned. There was a lovely person in there somewhere. She had just got lost.

Chapter Six

As the Autumn went on, Spring arrived. The effect of not living together all the time and regular sensible counselling began to work. There were signs of the person I knew and loved re-emerging. Vicky began to face the painful consequences, not just of her condition, which she couldn't help, but of her actions, which, up to a point, she could. She saw that the people she loved had been hurt. She also began to understand that everyone around her was not against her but actually trying to help get her through this process with an intact family.

For the first time in months I felt I could see our future together again. I wasn't kidding myself. We weren't through the tough stuff yet, after all we were still living apart, but Vicky I think, was beginning to see our separation as a temporary situation necessary to undo the damage caused previously. Sometimes she even seemed to understand that her step-daughter did still love her and even, sometimes, missed her. That understanding, transitory as it was, helped relieve the fear that fueled so much of her anger.

If it hadn't been for Vicky's terrible fear Ellie was lost to her, life might have begun to get back to normal, but she just could not leave it alone. Nor could she see the solution as in anyone's control other than Ellie. It was a terrible responsibility to lay at the door of a teenager. As much as she shouted, 'why can't she understand, nothing's changed, I'm the same' I wanted to shout back, 'everything has changed how could it be the same?'. These dual convictions, that Ellie was lost and only Ellie could put it right, were the hurricane that continued to tear through our family.

Ellie would open up to me about how distressed she felt to have lost the only father she ever felt proud of, and how much she missed him. She missed rock climbing with him, going to the movies, playing carpet football. These were huge huge steps and it required insight beyond her years to even begin to attempt them. I tried, more fool me, to share this with Vicky but her response was always the same - 'she hasn't lost anything, when is she going to understand that?'. What Vicky couldn't understand was that however many things she could still be to Ellie, Dad wasn't one of them.

My family certainly thought enough was enough. If Vicky wasn't willing to give anyone time to adjust to her reality, they were certainly giving her no more time to 'get it right' with Ellie or with me. Standing outside the situation, the solution seemed clear to them, and if I didn't see it, then I needed to have it explained to me.

My sister decided to explain it to me a week later. I had driven her husband and her to a local hospital where he was having minor surgery. Once he was admitted we went for for lunch. As we waited for our food to arrive my sister began to tell me how worried she was. Not so much for me, I was of course entitled to do whatever I wanted, but my children, specifically Ellie, because she was stuck in the middle of it all. For her, my sister was adamant, there was only one right answer. She was worried that I was putting my own happiness in front of my children's and, blinded by my false belief that Vicky loved me, was going to ruin my children's lives by 'forcing' them to accept her. I should have tried to explain to her that I didn't see accepting a transgendered step parent as a bad thing for my children, rather as a positive experience that would help them to become more open loving people themselves, I should have said that I didn't believe Vicky's love for me or the children, was false, but I didn't. I just sat there fuming with indignation, righteous or otherwise.

I pointed out in that over polite way that says, 'I'm only speaking like this because I don't have a baseball bat', that Vicky and I were still living apart, though we missed each other dreadfully, that we were attending counselling together and doing everything we could to allow Ellie to come to terms with what had happened in her own time. I'm sure she could hear the anger in my voice.

My refusal to hear what she was saying or consider that I might be mistaken only emphasized to her how trapped I was in the belief that there was a future with Vicky. That was where I was wrong. The question to her was clear. Why a previously devoted mother should be so willing to forget her children's well being could only mean that I was either unutterably selfish, and she wasn't willing to think that of me, or possibly mentally unstable, which she considered possible. All of this had been said to me because she really loved me, she was trying to be as gentle as possible, but enough. Leave Vicky for the sake of my children or she didn't feel able to continue having contact with me. Just as so many months earlier I had delivered my final trump card to Vicky, so my sister delivered it to me. If you really love me, you will leave.

I understand the sincerity of her concern and how painful it must have been to put everything we shared as twins on the line. I understand how genuinely worried she was. She could not see a way forward and she saw her much loved niece very distressed. Looking at it calmly from a distance I can see that. At the time I was furious. Outraged that she felt entitled to tell me how to live my life, how to raise my children, who I might love. But we were in a restaurant in Epsom and her husband was in surgery. I couldn't leave. Instead I sat there in undisguised fury. That was our lowest point. She had put everything she had on the line for me and I had refused to conform. We would not speak for another three months.

For some people not speaking to a sibling for three months would be a quite standard state of affairs. For my twin sister and me it was traumatic. Being a twin is like being married from the very beginning of your existence. When we were born my mother put us in separate cots but we wouldn't settle, finally she put us into the same cot and we apparently looked at each other as though to say 'oh, there you are'. It had always been like that. We had, of course, quarrelled our way through childhood, but were utterly loyal to each other. We briefly went our separate ways in our early twenties, more to establish our individuality than anything, but we spoke regularly, even if we didn't get to meet up. By the time our children arrived we made sure we saw each other nearly every day, and we certainly spoke every day. We ended up living very close to each other and felt we had the perfect arrangement. I was always there for her and she was always there for me. It is hard to explain to someone who isn't a twin, the closeness of the relationship, or the pain of feeling it was compromised.

A few days later my mother repeated the message to me as I was driving her home. Again, no way out, I was a captive audience. I was, she said, putting my own needs in front of my children, the definition of an unfit mother. I was very hurt and so angry I couldn't speak. When we got to her home I let her get out, slammed the door and drove off. Heavy on the accelerator. My mother is in her eighties, it wasn't an OK thing to do. I regret it, but I was only feeling my anger, it blanked out anything else. My mother had said she would never reject me, no matter how wrong my choices were. Right then it didn't seem much consolation.

So for the time being I had no support other than my friend Caroline who lived in Dorset. She gave me the best advice I have ever received. She said. 'They love you but they're angry and afraid. Don't buy into their drama'. No indeed, I had quite enough of my own. Don't buy into their drama. Step back and stop trying to control how other people feel. To these words of wisdom I added, 'It's all about the self', 'Life is a film not a photograph', 'keep speaking your truth'... These concentrated nuggets kept me going. The thing is, trite as they may seem, they are true. I had been doing all the things I was angriest at Vicky for. Trying to control how everyone felt and feeling let down when they had their own opinions. Ridiculous really.

My mother was very upset. The next day my sister told me over the phone, that my mother felt as though I had died. I suppose her image of me had been severely dented, but I didn't feel I had done enough to be considered dead. I sent her an email and tried to explain, to apologize, to make it right again. I wanted my mother's support and I was unused to not having it, but I couldn't base my decisions on it, I loved her but I also loved Vicky and I didn't want to have to choose. I'm sure that was a very unhappy time for my mother and I'm sorry I didn't have an instant solution. We would get there in the end but it was a strange time in all our lives, we were so used to functioning as a family that loved and accepted each other and then there was this. It didn't fit.

At the same time Ellie came to me and said she was ready to start calling Vicky, 'Vicky'. She had given it a lot of thought and saw this as the next step to moving on. I was deeply impressed that she had thought all this out herself. When children are tiny their knowledge of the world is so linked to your own understanding, and then bit by bit, almost imperceptibly they start working out their own ideas, their own view of the world. It's a miraculous process, like watching a butterfly emerging. Ellie was working this out, not because I had explained it to her, or told her how or what to think, but because she had her own thoughts on the subject. Well, I was amazed anyway.

My mum phoned me that evening and I told her again how sorry I was that she had been hurt. I had always been aware and indeed proud of how open minded my mother was. She challenged bigotry and prejudice wherever she found it. Suddenly I found my choices excluded from the list of things she would tolerate and I could not make sense of it. Especially as the reason I had the kind of heart and mind that could accept my husband becoming my wife, was because of her and the way she had brought me up. Well, when you think someone is wrong and they're making bad decisions, I guess you have to tell them. Especially if they're your daughter and you want their happiness very much. I don't think she could see my life with Vicky as a realistic outcome. What else could she have done? What else would I have done if it were my child making a decision I absolutely believed to be wrong?

Although there are some women who make it through their husband's transition with an intact functioning relationship, the vast majority do not and there's no getting away from that. Most who have chosen to commit to a relationship with a man do not want and are not able to have, a relationship with a woman. The heart wants what the heart wants. Many of those partners would not even see their transgendered partner AS a woman, but rather as a man suffering from some extreme form of mental delusion.

I posted this at the time, not that I expected anyone to come up with a solution.

> *The last week has been really really disappointing. My family, who I thought were behind us are, it turns out, behind me as long as I dump Vicky. I can't begin to describe how painful this is. My first clue was when my twin sister started ignoring any comments I made about things Vicky and I had done together. She would then simply continue talking about life as though Vicky had evaporated. My mum then decided to tell me that not only did she not trust Vicky because of how this situation has come about (Vicky suspecting she was trans but not telling me until after we were married) but now doesn't believe that Vicky ever loved me or loves me now. She also told me this is how my other sister feels and they are all concerned that I will 'weaken' and let Vicky move back in ignoring the unspeakable disaster this would be for Ellie and Rob.*
>
> *When I tried to say that Ellie is actually talking to me about her feelings and we are moving forward and of*

course both Vicky and I put Ellie's needs top of our list, she said 'things' were said in France (when Ellie was on holiday with my sister). Well I know what 'things' were said in France, and Ellie was perfectly entitled to say them and we are moving forward. My family seem to have decided on some marvelous sacrifice that I must make in order to still be a good mother. I must not see Vicky until Ellie leaves home, then, if I'm lucky, I'm allowed to try and start a relationship. In the meantime I should live as a single parent, steering Rob through his suicidal moments and steering Ellie through A levels and into university, and then sitting on my own in a corner until I am needed again.

I don't think so.

The bottom line is, as well as loosing all but one of my friends, again most will support 'me' but not 'us', I now lose my family. If I sound bitter, that is because I am. All I am doing is standing by the person I love in sickness and in health, better or worse etc etc, as promised. For this I am now dumped by my friends and family. Yes I can make new friends, but not a new mum or a new twin.

Looking back I cringe at the level of righteous self-pity I poured into every statement. My own feelings had become so much more important to me than anyone else's. I had in mind the response my family 'should' have been giving me. I had chosen a difficult life, staying with a transexual partner through transition, now I deserved unending support and understanding. Like a teenager trying to change a lightbulb, I waited for the universe to revolve around me.

Logically I could see that most people had a weaker imperative to find their way through the barriers because Vicky wasn't their partner, just a member of their extended family. Even Ellie said that ultimately this wasn't her life and she understood that the acceptance of someone as a life partner is different from the acceptance of someone as a step-parent. So it would probably take them longer, and, as we had found with some friends, that might mean never. The level of loss for them was on the scale of 'that's a shame, what's for dinner?'.

So much for the majority. I wanted to stay with the person I had married even with a new name and gender. I would sometimes repeat that sentence in my head and think 'how extraordinary, who would have guessed I would be ok with such a thing?', but I was. The bottom line was I loved this individual human being and I wanted to be with her, so I had to find my way through the barriers of expectation and conformity and remember what was important.

My family seemed to have decided that a happy relationship with me was possible as long as we didn't mention Vicky. Not a long term solution, but we would have to work that out in our own time. All I could do was not let myself get upset by their decision to 'never' see Vicky again and trust that 'never' was never as long as advertised.

I was certainly hoping it wouldn't last all the way to Christmas. I define myself as Christian, while my family are all atheists and Christmas had always been at my place. Faith aside I have always embraced festiveness with unashamed childlike excitement. Those around me have indulged my desire for cosiness and tinsel on an industrial scale, able to go safely to their own homes once they'd had enough. The best part had always been the gathering of family and friends. If I got wind that someone was looking at a solo December 25th I asked them to join us. The more the merrier. Now I write this down it seems rather intimidating, this deranged woman accosting every passing stranger like an over-reformed Scrooge, but I never gave anyone mulled wine and minced pies against their will. As far as I know. The thought of not being able to spend Christmas with all my family, and Vicky and my children was too awful to contemplate. How would that even be Christmas? Once again I found myself not in control and much as I tried to get it into perspective, my longing for everyone together and happy, was a physical ache I couldn't fix.

I looked at the post I made on line about this most painful subject, and noticed it was only mid-October. Like I said, Christmas is a big deal for me.

For a while there was a new life. It didn't involve daily contact with my sister, which I missed dreadfully. I really began to struggle with the isolation. My mother would call, but wouldn't come over if Vicky was going to be there. She would chat about anything but Vicky and talked about me as though I were single. It was loving but surreal. I had also lost contact with my oldest friend. She had been very honest and said she had tried to come to terms with knowing a transexual, but she just couldn't. I came as a pair that was no longer acceptable in her world, so what could either of us do. We too had been used to calling each other regularly and that too just stopped. What I didn't know was that she kept trying, and thinking and working it through. It was a long time before we made contact again, but we did and now that moment that seemed so permanent, like the Berlin Wall, is just a footnote in the history of our friendship. At the time though, I thought my friend was lost to me and it hurt like hell.

All this meant that on a daily basis I was alone. Only my children spoke to me, but of course that never involved Vicky or how I was feeling, and quite right too, your children are not the right people to dump your emotional struggles on. It was very lonely.

I felt like I was suffocating and no one even noticed. Or worse, maybe they did notice but they didn't care. We were in some hellish limbo, when Ellie and I both got flu, Vicky could only help by dropping groceries at the door. It was insane. I wanted my family back. It was an unusual family I'll grant you, a mother, a transexual step-parent, an autistic son and Ellie, but it was mine and I started to feel that if my family could have supported us and actively helped us to deal with the challenges, we would not be living apart now. Finding a home for my resentment I decided to try not caring what my family thought. I wasn't very good at it.

All this was confusing for Ellie who was being asked to accept Vicky while her extended family didn't. In fact they wouldn't speak to Vicky or acknowledge her existence. How, I wondered, was my child supposed to work this all out on her own in the face of such attitudes?

By the middle of November Vicky and I decided that I should talk to Ellie about ending the separation. Despite my efforts, she had been perfectly able to see how miserable I had been, and she no more wanted to sell our home and move away from the area than I did. Vicky was not a monster and she understood the behaviour of the summer had been temporary. She was willing to give it another go. So we all decided we were ready to try again.

On the 16th of November, Vicky came home. There were hugs and tears all round. We were a family again. Two days later I broke the news to my mother. She came over in the daytime while Vicky was out and she was not pleased. In her mind Vicky was no longer trustworthy. She was concerned that Vicky could 'turn' at any moment and might even physically harm Ellie or me. The extreme behaviour of the previous summer was the 'real' Vicky, and all this calm thoughtfulness an act. I think we managed a sensible discussion but we were obviously not going to agree. In the end she went to have tea with my sister nearby. They wanted me to join them but not with Vicky. It wasn't a hugely tempting offer. I'd already had a day of having my ill-judgement described in minute detail and I didn't fancy more of the same. Tea with a family who are nobly standing by you despite your unacceptable life choices is not as much fun as it sounds. Really. Imagine how much fun it is then halve it. It's less fun than that.

This would have made me miserable were it not for the fact that my family proper - Vicky and the kids and me - were a family again. My son had asked Vicky and me to take him to a Goth gig and Ellie seemed happier and relaxed with Vicky back home. That's all I had wanted, so why spoil it by being greedy and wishing for things that were out of my control?

Another partner of a transexual once described her memories of her husband as like a fondly remembered ex. At the time I found it hard to imagine being able to look at my wedding photos, or remember times we had spent together as husband and wife without the almost unbearable heartache that seemed to accompany such memories.

I decided I was ready to spend some time looking at a particular picture of 'us' before any of this had happened. We looked so very happy, our arms wrapped around each other, smiling like nothing could hurt us ever again. Knowing that somewhere inside Vicky was trapped changed some of that apparent happiness, but not all of it. We really had been in love, we really had found our souls mates. I'm not saying I didn't have a jolly good cry, remembering all the things I loved about 'him', but at the same time it was looking at someone who I had known, but I didn't know anymore. 'He' had died and I would never forget him. I would allow myself to remember 'him' and cry if I needed to, but I was also ready to embrace what I hadn't lost. I had put the picture on the mantlepiece over the last few weeks, but now I felt able to put it away with our wedding photos. That was my past, Vicky was my future. I had memories with 'him' and I would never forget them, but I was now building memories with Vicky that I could also look back on with happiness.

I think this was at least the beginning of genuine acceptance. There had been several false dawns, but this time it was real. I wrote online at the end of November:

Yes I want my Love to be happy and true to herself, but I loved the man she was and she didn't, so the happiness I thought we had was, ultimately, an illusion. The happiness we have now is the only happiness available, so there's no choice, and maybe that's why I sometimes feel angry and even cheated. I don't feel like I chose this life with all it' challenges - but I would rather this than lose my love.

Add into this the confusion of children, and Vicky often becomes overwhelmed with guilt at what she has 'done' to us. It's then I have to remind her that she didn't 'do' this to us, nature 'did' this to her and we face it as a family, as we would any other challenge.

Sometimes it's easy and everything feels very peaceful, other times I want my husband back and it makes me so very very sad, but the truth is I haven't lost my husband - she just went through a metamorphosis which she couldn't stop. Which is why my nickname for her is 'butterfly'

Unsurprisingly the butterfly is an international symbol for transgendered people. Maybe not just because a caterpillar becomes a butterfly, but maybe too because of the struggle involved in breaking free from the cocoon. To transition requires a huge amount of strength and persistence. I suppose if you know you're a butterfly it's no good staying in the cocoon, you have to fight free. It is eventually, an inspiring experience to watch someone break free. It is one of the things I love and admire about Vicky.

We lived quietly like this, getting back to normal, accepting the areas that were unresolved and healing from the year so far. About a week before Christmas a crisis hit. Suddenly what gender Vicky was became supremely unimportant. Far from being a problem she became a rock of support and that didn't go unnoticed. I don't know how we would have coped if it had happened 6 months earlier, we would have been in no position to be a help to anyone. The crisis involved several people very dear to me and it is not my story to tell, so I won't, but it focused our minds entirely elsewhere.

My mother rallied round and agreed to spend Christmas with us, despite her continuing reservations about Vicky. It made me very very happy to know she would be there, but my sister and her family would not come. We hadn't spoken for weeks and all information came through my mother. I didn't understand. We needed all hands on deck right then. I kept hoping that at the last minute they would change their mind and turn up. I promised my mother there would definitely be enough food if they did. Or they could come for tea. I know it's only a day, but it's amazing how it has the power to define how your life is going. If you're lonely, you'll be ten times more lonely on Christmas day. Everything gets magnified. Or maybe that's just me.

Our Christmas card count was suffering, despite my sending out a shed load. We were down to about twenty. I made the mistake of moaning about this online to the transgendered community and got a sharp reality check. People told me how they would be spending Christmas on their own, separated and ostracized from their entire families, parents, partners and children, who they were prevented from contacting. Suddenly my twenty Christmas cards seemed pretty damned wonderful. The online support group was such a necessary thing. Vicky and I now had each other, but so many people transitioned in complete isolation forced to lose everything and everyone from before they came out. Anyone who thinks you would 'choose' to bring such a fire storm down on yourself just so you could wear a skirt has seriously missed the point.

Christmas day came and we celebrated. Vicky's mother was also there. She had proved a bit of a dark horse. My own expectation had been that she wouldn't tolerate anything so far from her narrow Spanish-Catholic view of the world. When Vicky had gone over to her house to tell her I had waited to pick up the pieces following the 'you are no longer my child' speech. I knew that had happened to other transgendered people and I was braced. Instead she had told Vicky, 'you are my child and I will always love you'. She didn't understand why this was happening, I'm not even sure she really got what was happening, She thought, maybe even thinks, that her son liked dressing up in ladies clothes and wanted to play at being a girl. but that made her acceptance all the more important. It didn't stop her popping the odd masculine pronoun into conversation or telling her friends that the size 11 ladies heels in the hall were mine. Still, she never ever turned her back on us and for that, I thank her.

The one aspect of Vicky's transition that seemed to upset her was the name change. Why not Antonia? She wanted to know. It's a tricky one. Many transitioners do simply feminize their name, signifying, I suppose, that it's still them. Same sweetie, different wrapper,. For others, and Vicky was certainly one of those, the choice of a female name was a deeply personal statement about how they were not that male person. Not Anthony with an extra 'A' or a man with one less appendage.

I kept hoping my sister would drop by on Christmas day, but she didn't. One of my sister's best and worst characteristics is she is stubborn as a mule. She would tell you this is a quality we share and I would not disagree. She had said she wouldn't come for Christmas and she didn't. I shouldn't have been surprised. I was however very hurt. My mother stuck between two people she loved could do nothing. I shed tears over it and I told my mother that no matter what my sister did, what decisions she made I would never ever have done this to her. Then again, she's never done anything that worried me as much as she clearly found our situation, so I haven't ever had to prove that statement.

A year previously we had been living a lie. Pretending that Vicky wasn't Vicky. We had had months of real pain ahead of us and we had had no idea how hard it was going to be. We saw in 2010 together, we were ourselves, both of us. Vicky was well into her hormone treatment and her breasts were developing. She hadn't worn male clothes since August and everyone we knew, knew who we were. We had both screamed and shouted, we had questioned and struggled, but here we were, still a couple. We had received much counselling, much advice and much criticism. Still, we received it as Emma and Vicky.

Could we have done it better? There's an unanswerable question. I know couples who have been married for twenty-five years before one of them has admitted to being transgendered and others who are not even married yet, but trying to get there. Can you choose someone when they're not quite themselves yet? Ask anyone who fell in love as a teenager. We had been together for six years when Vicky spoke out. Would timing have made a difference. I suspect if on that first evening Anthony had said, 'by the way I expect to be undergoing corrective surgery soon because I'm actually a woman', I wouldn't have married her. My instinct says life without Vicky is unthinkable. It would certainly have been quieter.

Within the transgendered community the debate about when and indeed if to tell a sexual partner of your medical history, is not just a question of manners. Once a transgendered person has slept with someone and not mentioned their biological, social history, it is too late. Some do tell partners after this crucial moment, but the ones who do so in a public space are safer than the ones who do so in private, or worse still get 'outed' by some old photograph or bank statement accidentally discovered. It is dangerous to assume you know how another person will react. Statistically more walk away than stay at that moment, and a few do a lot worse. There's also the problem of men who would specifically like to date a transgendered woman. Not a problem if both parties are happy with that, but definitely a problem if it is insulting to be identified as fundamentally different from any other woman. Like being sought out because you've had a growth removed. "Tumors turn me on" is not a phrase any girl wants to hear, and also, "It turns me on that your vagina had to be constructed out of a penis" may not do it for everyone either. When I look at all the perils and pitfalls of dating for the transgendered woman, I think Vicky is luckier, and safer, with me.

Chapter Seven

After Christmas, I got a phone call from my sister. Would Vicky and I like to meet up for a coffee in a local coffee shop? We began to rebuild our relationship. At first rather self-consciously, but then more easily. We began popping into each other's houses again, sharing Saturday morning breakfasts. All of us. We never spoke about the things both of us had said in the restaurant in Epsom, or about the Christmas we had spent apart. I think it's better that way. We were both, in our own stubbornness, convinced we were right and there was only one way forward. We were both wrong. If you want to get your family across rough terrain, use a people carrier not a tank. Good advice which I gave to several others but never took myself. Youth may be wasted on the young, but wisdom is, in my hands at least, a huge waste of brain cells that could have been put to good use inventing chocolate that made you slimmer.

If you are anything like me you have now entirely stopped thinking about the complexities of living with a transgendered partner and are musing on the possibilities of prescription chocolate.

Anyway. The list of people who didn't want to know us anymore diminished daily, and the list of people who did was holding up nicely. I found myself looking at a wedding photo and thinking it looked like Vicky in a trouser suit. So far she had had no surgery and with the honourable exception of her breasts, might have been able to pass herself off as a man in the right clothes. Still, I saw her as Vicky and had no expectation that she would suddenly revert to 'being' a man.

We still went to counselling twice a week, Fridays, with Vicky's transition counsellor and Wednesdays with the relate marriage counsellor. Though sometimes there was a subject that still carried some heat, generally we would find ourselves chatting about our experiences quite calmly. Vicky was still waiting for her genital surgery date, now on the NHS because the financial and practical realities of private surgery in Thailand had put it out of reach for the moment.

In the meantime she was having speech therapy to help her 'lift' her voice in to a more feminine range. That was something of an uphill struggle as her voice had always been particularly dark and sonorous, more baritone than tenor. Despite all this in terms of daily life as a family and to the outside world transition had happened and we we're getting on with life as a trans couple. My son had completely accepted Vicky and was totally relaxed around her. Ellie was 99 percent there. She had been out for the day with both of us and though she still preferred Vicky in trousers, she didn't mind earrings and makeup being worn so everyone felt respected and accepted. Well, almost. I think Vicky was still looking for the magic happy ending in which everything had changed but nothing had changed. That certainly still carried heat and every now and then erupted into hurt angry confrontation. Part of that hurt was the loss of the ten year old girl she had first known. Ellie was growing up fast, she was, with the exception of housework, (like most teenagers a keen user of the floordrobe) more grown-up than child. I felt that loss too, but to Vicky it was so bound up with the timing of her transition, that she saw it as a direct consequence of it, rather than an unhappy coincidence. Believing she had triggered it, she thought she could fix it. Put it back as it had been. The last thing a teenager wants is to be pulled back to being a child and they continued to fizz and spar with tiring regularity.

Although my family was reunited and functioning, this didn't really mean we were all of the same opinion. By March my mother and sister and I were still trying to come to a common understanding of what the hell had happened. At the heart of this gap was the issue of being lied to and it continued to separate me from them in subtle ways. They reasoned that Vicky had known she was female from a very young age, as she had looked on the internet at how to transition, that she 'knew' transition was coming before she married me and therefore 'tricked me' into committing myself and my children to her. I could understand why they thought that, but I wanted to add, to mitigate this 'lie' with the fact that the first person Vicky lied to, was herself. Having made that lie it was impossible she could have told me anything else. A huge huge damn of self denial which had taken the whole last year to work through with therapy and many many tears. How she was supposed to explain to me that she was transgendered before she understood it herself I couldn't see, and I couldn't see why they couldn't see it.

Of course the consequence of all this self delusion was that she wasn't able to prepare me for the news, and once she'd told me, much like a damn bursting, there was no holding back, waiting or giving me time to adjust. The plans that my sister and I had made when I first told her of Vicky's condition, and the plans that my mother had made which ultimately saved Vicky and my relationship, were not, of themselves, achievable. With an avalanche the only choice is when to clap your hands, after that it's pretty much going at the speed it's going. That first year, post hand clap had been pretty bloody awful, but we got through and here we were, quietly getting on with our life as a devoted couple, facing all the same challenges as every other married couple, and a few extra ones that weren't in the handbook. My family were supporting us, but that nagging doubt that Vicky could and should have done things differently remained for some time as an unresolved thorn in all our sides.

By May, Victoria was on her way to Los Angeles to photograph an off-road racing competition. I dropped her at the airport in the morning, she was looking very feminine and business like, though she hadn't had time to do her make-up, nonetheless she looked good. She was wearing a pair of corduroy slacks, a coffee coloured knitted top, rather thirties with a bow motive and a bright purple three quarter length raincoat. So much better than the clothing choices she was making six months ago, she looked positively elegant. At check-in the woman behind the desk twice called her 'sir' despite Vicky correcting her the first time and despite the rather obvious fact that she had a passport in the name of Ms Victoria etc etc. It does make you wonder why, if they thought she was a man 'disguised as a woman' traveling with a woman's passport, why they weren't calling security and escorting 'him' from the building, or to the nearest police station. If, as the provision of a boarding pass indicated, they accepted this was indeed Ms Victoria Cantons, why on earth did they think it was polite to call her 'sir'?

I wish I could have done something. I wish I could have stormed down there and demanded they treat her properly. Life was hard enough as a pre-operative transexual without this stupid woman's extra layer of dumb judgement. Is it really so much to hope that a first world society could try treating everyone with whom it comes into contact with consideration and respect? Even if they are unusually tall for a woman? Like smiling, politeness is cheap and rarer than it needs to be.

I know it's really important not to get paranoid, but it does seem when part of the interaction involves a passport with a female identity, that any possible confusion should be gone. To then address a customer as sir in direct contradiction of the document in their hands seems to have at least an element of deliberate rudeness.

It is in the little almost imperceptible actions that our society defines itself. The subtle accidental 'sir'-ing of a transgendered woman is much harder to confront than it's less subtle cousin - the transphobic comment - but they are the same family and should always be challenged. Both equally dehumanise and that is never a good thing.

Vicky was planning what surgery she was willing to undergo. The genital surgery may seem to the outsider the most blindingly obvious requirement, but it was not the one that would cause the biggest difference to Vicky's interaction with the rest of the world. There was no prospect of that happening for at least another year anyway, treatment protocols being what they were, and so she turned her attention to the two other areas that could, at a price, be changed. Her voice, and her face.

Firstly, she was being referred for vocal surgery. Despite having worked really hard at speech therapy, there was no getting round the thickness of her vocal chords, so this was her only way forward. Her vocal chords needed to be tighter. The procedure would not involve any cutting of the vocal chords, but instead the pulling apart of the cartilage that held them, which in turn would stretch the vocal chords and raise their overall pitch. The other surgery Vicky wanted to get 'out of the way' before her final operation, was facial. She wanted to go the whole nine yards. Brow reduction, cheek implants, jaw reduction, face lift, nose job, lip lift, you name it, she wanted it.

I found the thought of this deeply deeply traumatic. I understood that she wanted to look as feminine and attractive as possible, but we had only just found our balance as a family after a pretty hairy year and Ellie had only just begun talking about her feelings around 'loosing' her step-dad. This all seemed horribly familiar, the demanding toddler voice shouting, 'give it NOW'.

She made what I thought was an initial enquiry phone call to the face surgeon in Chicago (whose name I cannot spell so don't ask me!!) . Twenty minutes later she excitedly announced she had a provisional date for surgery in 12 weeks time. Back to square one I thought. Once again we were shouting at each other, if you really loved me you would understand, if you really loved me you would wait. I was not happy.

She seemed oblivious to the challenge that radically altering her face would present to the rest of us. I had thought this surgery was about two years away and suddenly it was in a matter of weeks, and in Chicago. I was going to be expected to be there supporting and looking after Vicky, who would doubtless be in extreme pain and pretty helpless. Who was going to look after me? It felt like once again, Vicky had decided what she wanted and that it was impossible for her to wait another second. Avalanche.

In my mind the genital surgery was a necessity, but the face surgery was about a subjective belief that she wouldn't look good enough without it. I respected her right to make that choice, but I also wanted, no insisted, she at least consider the impact on everyone around her. Our faces are our trademarks, instantly recognizable as us and no one else. Change that and how are you to be still yourself? How are your family to still see the child they raised the partner they love, the parent they rely on. It's a big ask. This was just a tell.

I really thought Vicky had got to a more stable place from where she was in that first year, but this sounded like a very backward step. There was a level of panic in her decision making process a sort of 'now or never' which was once more bringing out the bulldozer instead of the people carrier.

It also seemed to demand my continuing role as logistics manager, trying to bring everyone else along with us as Vicky rushed headlong in to her glorious future with never a backward glance. Did I have the emotional strength to support the children through another radical change quite so soon after everything else. Let alone come to terms with how I might feel about my partner undergoing such a large amount of surgery and having to get used to a very different face from the one I knew. I don't think any of this has even crossed Vicky's mind. I was especially worried about my son, his autism made change very difficult for him to process. He had done so magnificently with the news that his step-father was female, but how could he process someone who just looked utterly different. What if he just couldn't 'know' Vicky anymore.

Then, at the end of May, right in the middle of all this agonizing over the timing of surgery, my son stepped into the road near his college without so much as a sideways glance. He was hit by a lorry. He flew through the air, was knocked unconscious and his bottom lip and chin were badly damaged. I got a phone call as I was on my way to visit my father in Ruislip. I drove to the Gloucester hospital not knowing anymore than that he had not been conscious when he was taken to hospital. When I got there he was having his chin stitched back together. I tried to hold his hand but nearly fainted and had to wait outside. Useless bloody mother. Afterwards, unable to speak, his face swollen and bruised, he stretched his arms out for a hug. Autistic people are not big on hugging, it was, I think the third hug he had ever given me. I brought him home and we fed him baby food and crushed up painkillers drunk through a straw. This, I thought to myself, is what Vicky wants to do to herself on purpose. She will make her face even more damaged than this and for what? To appease a society that can't understand not everyone gets born just so? It seemed to me very wrong. If society can't handle your face surely what needs to change is society.

My beautiful boy was miraculously ok. No broken bones and, two weeks later, his face looked as though nothing had happened apart from a very cool scar on his chin, which many a goth would have paid good money for. He still maintained it was the lorry driver's fault, but it was a forty mile an hour zone and the driver had been doing twenty five. I thank him with all my heart. After two weeks he was well enough to go back to college on the firm understanding that there was a bit more work to do on road safety. We lived to fight another day.

Something was wrong with Vicky. She had got what many a transexual dreams of, a loving and supportive family, normality, and yet she was miserable. Looking at the problem sensibly it became clear that its cause was chemical not emotional. Maybe her hormone treatment was causing her problems. She went for blood tests in August, thanks to our GP who was being brilliant. Vicky was, essentially, depressed. Why she was depressed needed to be looked into. There were several possible culprits, but the spring had gone out of her step and she couldn't see the positives about her anymore. She was also suffering from night sweats - quite severe, it was like sleeping next to a swimming pool. Oh yes,and hot flushes. She was like a menopausal woman, except transition was supposed to be like puberty. It really did seem a bit unfair that my 'husband' had hit the menopause before me.

Alongside all this Vicky had booked her FFS (facial feminization surgery) for the middle of October in Chicago which meant I would be able to be there for the first week and hold her hand. After that I had to get back to be there for my children. A few months after that she would have the vocal surgery to tighten her vocal chords and raise her voice pitch. Now we believed that the GCS wouldn't be until the following autumn and then, oh then, it would all be done and we could get on with the rest of our lives. No more surgery to face, no more transition, just years and years of nothing much. It sounded lovely.

Vicky was about to prove herself the noblest of step-parents. For months her step-son had been going on about a weekend Goth festival called 'Bloodstock'. I know. It sounds delightful, I'm surprised you haven't been. Anyway I had kind of volunteered to go, in a tent and stay in the middle of non-stop grinding goth metal music with my darling child for four days. I was quite worried about how I would cope. It was at this point that Vicky, in an act of beautiful self sacrifice and love, offered to go instead. To a Goth festival for four days. Four days in a tent with an autistic 20 year old who couldn't stop talking. They say worse things happen at sea. I doubt it. I determined that, should she survive, I would buy her the shiniest sparkliest, most inappropriate shoes I could find. I felt genuinely guilty as I waved them off with their camping gear. Just not quite enough to take her place. It was about this time that Son came up with alternative lyrics to the 'Addams family' theme tune:

A step-dad who's transgender
A son who plays a Fender
A mum who can't remember
The Cantons family.

I was left to have a lovely mother daughter weekend with my gorgeous girl which I was really looking forward to. We might not have been average, but we were happy.

Finally blood test results showed Vicky had an underactive thyroid which accounted for all sorts of odd symptoms she had been suffering from. Aside from the depression, there was hair loss and dry patches of skin on her hands, not to mention the difficulty she had experienced in shifting weight despite exercising like a mad thing. This was particularly important with major surgery coming up. Once Vicky was reassured that she was not going mad but just suffering the well known effects of a thyroid condition she actually started doing a lot better at regulating her anger, which made it nicer for everyone around her! All treatable thank goodness.

My remaining concern was that, despite our best efforts, there was no one to come to Chicago with us for Vicky's eight hour facial surgery. I would have to sit that one out on my own and the prospect of it frightened me. In my darkest moments I imagined something going wrong and finding myself having to phone my mother in law and tell her her child was dead. I did not want to be alone. I also could not begin to imagine what Vicky would look like. Immediately of course, she would look like she'd been attacked with a baseball bat, but later, when the swelling had gone down. Would she still look hispanic, like a member of her family? Would there be anything left that I could recognize of the person that I'd fallen in love with? There just wasn't any way of knowing. I think Vicky was scared too, but she wasn't letting on.

It was hard for both of us. Some people have suggested to me that it is harder for a partner. I think it's hard but I have no idea what it is like to be transgendered. I think maybe one difference for a partner is that you have a choice which your transgendered partner doesn't. You can leave. Choosing not to leave can bring down the wrath of family and 'friends' who think they know better than you what you should do. It's that element of choice, especially if you have kids, that makes other people feel entitled to shun you when you don't do what they think is best. That is hard. For everyone.

The American surgeon came to London to meet with all of his prospective English patients. The event, and it felt like an event, took place in London. A combination of past and prospective patients, it was the largest number of transgendered women I had ever met. There was a private meeting with Doctor. D. where we were shown the physical realities of what could be achieved, grinding down bone and repositioning skin and cartilage. We asked lots of questions and learnt a lot of things I'd rather not have known about plastic surgery. I can see why Vicky would put herself through this, but I will certainly be growing old as nature intended, saggy and wrinkly. Gorgeous.

After the one on one meetings we gathered for a presentation with slide show, showing past patients, some of whom were actually there. We met Sarah, a young transgendered woman with both her parents there. Due to go over to Chicago in a few weeks time, she was slim and gentle but her face was so masculine, prominent

117

Adam's apple, large pointy nose, obvious masculine jaw and brow. I felt so sad for her and all that she would have to face presenting as female, but looking so obviously male. Still she had the love and support of her parents and that was wonderful, Maybe it would be enough.

Some of the transgendered women were fervent in their support of Doctor. D. The transformations he had achieved for them were almost unbelievable. First we would be shown the picture of a transgendered woman, looking no more female than Sylvester Stallone, then the 'after' picture, they were not all beautiful, though some were, some of them were plain, but they were all female, and they looked happy. Beautiful men, I realized, make beautiful women, and plain men make plain women. You can switch your perceived position on the gender continuum, but not on the beauty line. There, your position is fixed. It was quite a realization. I am as beautiful as I will ever be and as I ever was, no more and no less. Age won't have anything to do with it, I will be this level of lovely (or not, Vicky thinks I'm beautiful and that's enough for me) whatever I look like. What a strange way to learn such a lesson. What I really understood at that meeting though, was that this was really going to happen, Vicky was going to be one of those 'after' shots. How would I even recognize her?

It was the beginning of October. Vicky was only two and a bit weeks away from facial feminization surgery in Chicago. It was estimated that it would take eight hours to complete the operation, maybe longer.

Ellie had begun telling more and more friends about her step parent, most were lovely and not bothered at all, but one day she came and told me that one person she had spoken to had elected to tell everyone he knew in the 'OMG' style, that there was a 'tranny' living in the area. Once he knew it was a transexual and her step-parent, the boy refused to speak to her. He and his friends had, according to her, been having a good laugh at her expense. Though you might argue such a boy was no great loss as a friend, it was very upsetting. I felt so useless. Unable to undo the hurt that had been caused to her or stop such cruel behaviour by young people I'd never even met.

The timing was awful. I was completely torn between wanting to stay and help Ellie deal with such a horrible situation and the knowledge that if I didn't go to Chicago in a couple of weeks leaving Ellie to handle all this on her own, Vicky would be amongst strangers at one of the most difficult moments of her life. My consolation, and really the saving of the situation, was that my twin sister reassured me she would be there if needed for Ellie.

I also talked to Ellie about the difference between being a prat and hate crime. I explained to her that she didn't have to put up with taunts anymore than she would if it were racially motivated or to do with sexual orientation, I was still worried though. It was a lot for a 17 year old to deal with. Even when she had found it hard, she always knows what was right and stood up for her step parent in the face of such nastiness.

As she said to me one morning, 'you can't have everyone arrested who isn't nice to me'. Well no, even over protective me realized that! On the other hand, I didn't want her to accept transphobic abuse as just 'one of those things'.

Vicky and I went to Chicago. At the airport she showed her passport. The next time she showed her passport in this country she would need a doctor's letter to confirm it really was her.

Chapter Eight

'Chicago'

We arrived in Chicago in the middle of October. Well, close to Chicago. The Sears Tower, once the tallest manmade structure in the world, was just visible on the horizon from our hotel window. I covered it with one thumb. If only all manmade structures were so easily removed. The testosterone that had coursed through Vicky's body all her life had certainly done a lot of damage. Ending up with the wrong genitalia was the most obvious problem, but there were many others. The thickening of the brow bone, the jaw, the flattened cheek bones, an Adam's apple, all these things gave her an obviously masculine appearance. There were subtler things too. The distance between the bottom of the nose and the top lip is shorter in females. You may not think you are aware of such things, but evolution has programmed all of us to constantly make this same assessment again and again. Male or female, potential partner or potential threat?

We were met at the hotel by a member of the surgeon's staff called Lisa. She was petite and the closest to bottled sunshine I have ever met in a human being. We both liked her immediately. This was a good thing because Lisa had been engaged to provide twenty four hour care for Vicky for the week post-op. She would sleep on the couch in our hotel room for the first week, and in one of the twin beds for the second week, after I had gone back to London.

Lisa drove us to the clinic, chatting all the way. She had supported many transgendered women through their facial feminizing surgery and was ready with the answers to a dozen questions we hadn't even thought about yet.

At the clinic we met Doctor D. again. He was a human whirlwind of energy and I began to see why the English and the

120

Americans have always had such complex emotions about each other. I'm sure he found us bemusingly unenthusiastic to the point of rudeness, but then I found him equally hard to take, his brash self-confidence more appropriate in my eyes to a used car-salesman than a skilled surgeon who was about to take Vicky's face apart and rebuild it according to his own beliefs about what was 'good'.

I suppose I had been raised on a diet of paternalistic English doctors, who had decided the general public, bereft of a medical degree, must all be gibbering fools. I expected to be talked down to, quietly, and allowed, if I were good, to have some treatment. Doctor. D. Was quite clear goodness had nothing to do with it. Can you afford it, do you want it and do I think I can do it. Yes? Well all right then. He was also refreshingly open about the risks involved. What could go wrong, with operations in general, anaesthetics and all that, but also what could go wrong with facial surgery, loss of sensation, loss of sense of smell, taste and so on, infections, tissue rejection, oh yes, and death. Death is always a risk with any general anaesthetic, medical teams do everything they can do avert it, but ultimately, it's a gamble and you went into this with your eyes open. The surgery would make Vicky look more conventionally female, it could not guarantee beauty. If he could do that, Doctor D. told us, he'd be a millionaire.

The first thing to do was take some photo's of Vicky so we could compare and contrast afterwards. She was at the moment, so to speak, the crumbling kitchen with out of date boiler and 70's decor, any minute now it would be all chrome and glass splash-backs. Doctor. D. talked Vicky through everything she would need to do pre-op, and everything she would have to do post-op if she wanted a good outcome. One thing I liked very much about Doctor. D. He always referred to me as Vicky's 'Honey'. I liked that. Not wife, not partner, but something to sweeten her life.

Doctor D. Looked at the pictures Vicky had paid to be computer generated, giving a possible outcome to surgery. He was confident he could do better and that Vicky would still look like a member of her family, like Anthony's sister. He showed us some photographs of a young transgendered lady we'd met at his conference in London called Sarah. She was only a few months post surgery but she looked amazing, no, she looked beautiful. A beautiful young woman who would go into the world and live a normal life. How wonderful.

The major challenge was going to be the speed of healing because of the under-active thyroid condition. It would take longer for the swelling to go down, but how much longer was difficult to predict. Even in normal circumstances it could take up to a year for a nose to return to its fully unswollen condition. The jaw line might well take close to that to emerge and the eyes were anyone's guess.

I'm sure Vicky felt a pang of regret looking at the pictures of that young woman. What might her life have been like had she been able to transition at 20? The myriad of problems that could have been avoided by being always recognised as a woman, never having to 'tell' people, to go through the whole battle for acceptance, loosing friends, work, being jeered at in the street. Surely it would be a lot better if all transgendered people could get the treatment they needed early. Part of that would be about public acceptance of the condition, so that a person wouldn't have to be afraid to say, 'I think I might be the wrong gender'. On the other hand the emotional challenge that acknowledging oneself as transgender presents, is not one I would want to face at twenty. Maybe sometimes it is better to wait til you have the emotional maturity to cope. I suppose that is an individual's decision and you can't legislate for it either way.

Once the photos had been taken we were dispatched to a nearby clinic under the confident care of Lisa, to get Vicky's blood tests. America really does look like the movies. All the houses look like film sets and the police are in costume. The outskirts of Chicago look ripe for a Spielberg coming of age drama, all wide avenues and clapboard porches. Golden Retriever ownership may be a state requirement for all I know, there were certainly enough of them.

Next to the supermarket which was the size of Dorset and contained a huge pharmacy that would have made more sense as a large high street shop rather than plonked next to the fruit and vegetable stands. With Lisa's guidance we stocked up on cotton gauze squares, sterile eye-drops, various gels and unctions for spreading on Vicky's post-operative face and a baby feeding spoon, because that, apparently, was the biggest thing she'd be able to get in her mouth. It was all pretty alarming, but Vicky had her eye on the prize and nothing was going to put her off now.

We also stocked up on food, for though the hotel had a restaurant, our room had a small kitchen, and I was determined to help Vicky's recovery as much as I could with some proper home cooked food. I couldn't work out what the various cartons of milk were in terms I might understand. 4%? , 6%? Fat, I assumed, but did that make it the creamiest liquid known to mankind or little more than white tap water. I asked Lisa which one was semi-skimmed. What, she wanted to know, did that mean? Two nations divided by a common language. Anyway, I got milk. I think it was a bit creamier than we normally used. It may have been cream.

Cucumbers. Cucumbers are an entirely different object in the U.S. Bumpy thick skinned things, looked more like courgettes, which as I'm sure you know, aren't courgettes but zuchinni..or is that aubergine? I had certain issues shopping in America. Luckily I wasn't planning on making my legendary cucumber and courgette skimmed milk custard, so it didn't matter.

Finally we went back to the hotel and flopped. It had been a long day. The next morning we went down to breakfast, which was a combination of very good and deeply upsetting to the entrenched Englishwoman who doesn't drink coffee and expects marmalade as a human right. There was porridge though and fruit, which may have been placed there for decorative purposes, but I put it to better use.

It had been suggested that we might like to go into Chicago to do some sight-seeing. I found the idea very strange. This was not a holiday and to wander around Chicago as though it were, would have been to ignore the reality of imminent, life-changing surgery. Nothing could have been further from our minds. Both of us just wanted to get this safely over and done with. Being so far from home gave the whole thing a disconnected quality. Also being surrounded by people who were completely at ease with having a transgendered woman in their midst. The hotel regularly supported post-operative recovery and they had no trouble getting Vicky's gender right. In my head everything had gone on hold. I was so wrapped up with the necessity of getting to grips with how the hotel worked, where the shops were, what time meals might be available, I couldn't think of anything else.

My aunt, wise wise woman, once had my cousin then a teenager, say to her, 'I'm so wrapped up with my work I can't think of anything else'. Her reply was, ' I wonder what the anything else is that you can't face thinking about?'

Well exactly. Focussing on getting the right skimmed milk blotted out the awful thought that the face I had fallen in love with, was about to go. I would never see that nose again, or that chin, or, anything I recognised. My wedding photos would show someone who physically no longer existed. Would this be the moment at which Anthony finally died, and not accidentally, but quite deliberately with pre-purchased eye-drops and baby feeding spoons? I had no control over this, though Vicky frequently asked me if it was still OK to have the surgery. What was I going to say? 'No, I insist you spend the rest of your life being mistaken for a man and jeered at for believing you are female'. How could I, could anyone else, have the right to determine such a thing?

A thought occurred to me that cheered me up. The eyes would be the same. A thing that had not changed through all the changes. I could look into those eyes and still see the person I had fallen in love with and still loved. In every other respect the person who was going to emerge from the surgery in 24 hours time, was going to be utterly unrecognizable. So I focussed on her eyes. I'll know you, I thought. Even under all those bandages.

There was lots of to-ing and fro-ing the day before surgery. Lots of checks and tests, forms and instructions. We had an enormous folder full of instructions of what to do post surgery. How to ensure the best possible outcome. If things didn't end up looking as good as they could, it would be Vicky's fault for slacking on her self-care.

The day went and it was evening. Vicky was going down to the clinic at five in the morning, to be collected from the hotel by Lisa. I was not invited. My job was to wait until I got a call saying Vicky was out of surgery and then I should come down to the clinic to help bring her back to the hotel. So I would wave her off at 5am the next morning and that would be the last time I would see that face. Oh yes, and no crying. That was my own rule but I had no idea how I was going to do it.

We sat in the hotel room watching rubbish TV, with which most channels were generously stocked, then there was a knock at the door. I opened it to find a slim middle aged transgendered lady standing outside. Her name was Angelique and she had just arrived. She was due to have her facial surgery the day after Vicky and she had come to give us a bit of support.

Angelique's life had been very hard indeed. She had once saved up the money for her surgery but before she could book in had been so viciously attacked on the street that she had had to spend all the money on medical expenses. Her family had rejected her, she had struggled to find work, or love, or kindness. Our lives seemed absolutely blessed by comparison. The things we fretted about bore no comparison to the challenges Angelique faced every day. She was here on her own, no support and she was uncomplaining. She was the kindest, gentlest person and she wanted to look like a film star. Well, why not? There are worse things to dream about.

Angelique decided I should not have to be alone to see Vicky off at 5am and determined she would be there to hold my hand. I was so relieved to discover at the eleventh hour that I would have someone to talk to while Vicky was in surgery.

We phoned home, everyone said good luck, call us when it's over. We checked Vicky's bag for the hospital, everything was in order and we went to bed.

At 4am the alarm went off. Vicky was already awake, I think she'd been lying awake for some time. She told me, not for the first time, that if I wasn't able to cope with this that she would back out. I know she meant it, but really once you are living life as a woman, dressing and speaking and expecting to be identified as a woman, walking around with a square jaw and manly brow can only make life harder, for everybody. I knew this operation would make life easier for both of us, and maybe would help people see the truth of who Vicky really was. Vicky didn't want to look monstrous, I just wanted her to be safe. We went down to the foyer and waited for the car to arrive.

Angelique was there, bless her heart. I don't think I've ever been so relieved to see someone keep their promise. The car came and we waved Vicky off. I nearly cried, but Angelique gave me a big hug and said, 'Right, lets get some breakfast'. It was just what I needed, no big fuss but lots of support.

After breakfast we decided to go to a huge shopping mall about half an hours drive away, where I could get a 'get well soon' balloon and other things that Vicky was unlikely to be able to see for the first 48 hours. Still, I wanted to do it, so that when she could open her eyes, there would be something to smile about.

We eventually found a card and balloon shop where I got a card and a butterfly shaped balloon for Vicky. All pink I'm afraid, whatever other improvements in her sartorial decision making there had been, her allegiance to pink was undiminished.

Every hour or so I would get a call from the surgeon, a thing I had not expected, telling me that the chin or neck or whatever was all done and they were moving on to the nose, eyes, brow, etc. Vicky was doing great and all was well. I have to admit part of me wanted to say, as to the pilot who starts mingling with the passengers, 'shouldn't you be, um, flying the plane?' so to speak. I was, nevertheless very grateful to have these regular updates. It was strange too to know the exact moment at which Vicky's face altered forever. 'He' was going, inch by inch, feature by feature. It seemed to be taken as read that, as I was there, I was good with it all. Supportive, loving and untouched by regret. No, they couldn't have been that dumb. They must have known what I was going through, but what use would it have been to start talking about it? That would have to be some other time.

There was a strange disconnection that day. My husband's face was being removed from my partner. The last two years were being given physical form, everything had been leading to this irreversible conclusion and I was wandering a round a Chicago shopping mall with a transgendered lady I'd only met 12 hours ago looking at tropical fish swimming around inside an armchair. Well I suppose if your husband can turn out to be a woman, why shouldn't they put goldfish in furniture. Normality is an illusion and conformity not all it's cracked up to be. Better to float along the river than try and swim against it all the time. It was also much better than sitting in a hotel room on my own worrying myself sick with no information.

Angelique and I found our way, not only out of the mall, but to the right car-park, which believe me was an achievement. We drove back to the hotel to wait for the call telling me to come in and collect Vicky. We waited and waited. The 8 hour operation had now taken 11 hours. I knew she was alright because I'd had the regular updates, but I couldn't understand why I hadn't been asked to come in yet. Finally Angelique, whose own operation was the next day, decided we should go in anyway and wait in the reception area. Better there than pacing about an empty hotel room.

The staff were slightly nonplussed to see me there quite so early, but they went and told the surgeon I was outside. Lisa came out in surgical scrubs, she had been assisting with the operation. Everything had gone wonderfully she told me. Vicky was in recovery but I would have to wait out here. She went back in and I sat obediently in the waiting area. A few moments later she came out again, not to invite me in, but to say that Vicky was rather distressed. This sometimes happened with anaesthesia but it might take a little longer until she calmed down. She went back in.

The third time she came out she was looking slightly puzzled. 'We're not quite sure why', she told me,' but Vicky is meowing'. Immediately I relaxed, meowing, I knew, was quite normal in our household. Friendly morning greetings, sorry I was grumpy, I'm really happy, all these and more could be and regularly were, communicated in our family with a simple 'meow'. Vomit all you like, that's how we are. Sometimes on school runs we worked our way through the Led Zeppelin back catalogue entirely in meows. Ellie Vicky and I all meowing away with never a blush.

Obviously Vicky was disorientated and in pain, of course she was meowing. "just let me come and hold her hand', I said, 'we meow a lot'. I was led through to the recovery room. Vicky was lying on a gurney wrapped in bandages and wadding so that her face was, barring a triangle of eyes and mouth, utterly covered. She was indeed, meowing. 'Meoooooowwww', she cried. 'I'm here darling, meow meow, it's all over, you're safe. Mow mow.' Vicky immediately became calm. Lisa was astonished, apparently meowing is not as common post operatively as we would have thought. The surgeon came in to see how Vicky was doing, and was very pleased to find everything calm at once. 'We need to make a note of that meowing thing' he said, 'that's one for the journals'.

He was pleased too with how Vicky was looking. Either he was one of life's 'glass half full people', or I had missed something. She did completely resemble a bowling ball, round and shiny and entirely the wrong size for a head. Her eyes were swelled shut and her lips looked not so much bee stung as swarm attacked. We gently helped her into a wheelchair and sat with her while she adjusted to being upright. I would not have been in Angelique's shoes for any money. As we wheeled Vicky through the reception area to the car, she could see the full horror of this very recent surgical procedure. Tomorrow it would be her.

We drove back to the hotel and Vicky was helped by Lisa and myself into her wheelchair. The staff at the desk smiled and congratulated Vicky as we passed them, they had seen this many times before and were not in the slightest bit fazed. It was nearly Halloween and we looked good and ready.

In the room we got Vicky into bed and Lisa began the hourly application of moisturisers and lubricants that would be necessary over the first week to aid her recovery. Keeping the eyes moist and sterile was particularly important. Thank God for Lisa, I can't begin to imagine how I would have begun to do this without guidance. I was terrified of hurting Vicky, she was in so much pain already, and that was in spite of a hefty range of pain killers. Her eyelids, that had less skin than before and were in a different position had to be kept wet constantly, drops had to be somehow got onto her eyeballs, which, so far, were completely swollen shut. Her ears were also swollen shut, her nose filled with wadding which would remain in place for the next 48 hours. She couldn't open her mouth, and she could only drink through a straw. There were so many things that needed doing in just the right way and they were all covered in the hefty handbook, but much like having a baby, there is no book yet written that can prepare you for the reality. As I said, thank God for Lisa.

We helped Vicky to the bathroom. She could barely stand and needed both of us to manouvere her onto the loo. She could barely communicate either, which wasn't surprising, but working out that she wanted a drink, or that her pillows were hurting her was tricky.

Finally, at about ten o'clock in the evening Lisa told me to go to bed, she would do the night shift, getting up on the hour every hour and applying eye drops and anything else Vicky needed. I would need to take over for part of the day so that she could get a few hours sleep. How anybody does that when it's not their own baby I don't know. When I had my son he was, to put it mildly, a poor sleeper. For the first year of his life he preferred the 10 minute cat nap to any of that boring all night nonsense. I was exhausted and when my husband was away for work my twin sister offered to come and stay the night, sharing the night shift with me, letting me sleep for at least some of it. At midnight she turned to me and with utter confidence announced, 'I am here for you'. She then fell immediately asleep and didn't stir, despite my baby's best efforts, until 7am. She was mortified but I think that's completely normal and I have no idea how Lisa found the energy to keep going the way she did.

I climbed into bed, exhausted and grateful that it was all over. I thought to myself, my husband is gone and I will never see him again, Anthony is no more. Then, as quietly as I possibly could, I cried myself to sleep.

I was crying for many reasons, not least tiredness. I was crying for all the pain Vicky was in, and all the pain we had gone through as a couple to get to this point. I was crying for myself because I wanted someone to hug me and look after me, to tell me it would be all right. I was crying because my lovely Anthony was gone and I would never see him again. I'm crying as I write this, because that pain, that sadness will never leave me, anymore than the sadness over the death of my brother. Every now and then I will still sit down, remember and have a good cry. It doesn't mean I don't accept the situation. My brother came off his bike at 70mph, hit by a car. That isn't something you can survive. Death was inevitable. Anthony should never have been called Anthony, she was female all along, this had to happen, it was the right thing. Vicky had to get her body put right, and if I really loved her, I would want her to get her body put right too. I did really love her, it's just I really loved him too, and his loss hurt.

The next morning I awoke to find Lisa quietly tending to Vicky. I got up and dressed quickly and quietly then went and sat in the living room. Vicky was sleeping. Drugged up to the eyeballs, it wasn't surprising, but I hadn't expected the days to be so quiet post surgery. Lisa and I sat drinking tea and waited for Vicky to wake up. When she did we helped her to the bathroom again, plumped up her pillows and washed her eyes and lips. She couldn't speak but would hold her thumbs up to let us know she was fine. Well as fine as a swollen bowling ball could be.

Doctor. D. arrived to examine her. He came in his usual whirlwind of energy, and asked me to take pictures as he removed the bandages, so that Vicky could examine them later and get an idea of how she was looking. This moment that I had dreaded for so long, was not going how I had imagined. I had seen myself asking Vicky to remove the dressings while we were on our own, giving me time to take in each alteration, one by one, at my own pace. Silly really, why I thought we would be allowed to do such a thing. As far as Doctor. D. was concerned, I was part of the care team and my feelings didn't enter into it. Vicky would want to see photographs, he and Lisa had their hands full removing the dressings, I was just standing there, why shouldn't I take the pictures.

So I did, recording bit by bit as the bandages came off and Vicky's new face was revealed. She looked horrific. Stitched and swollen, the victim of some terrible attack. I could see that her nose was now a gentle slope, and her brow was utterly different, smaller, flatter. Her eyes were impossible to gauge. There were so many stitches. Her ears looked like they had been taken from someone else and stitched onto her head as an afterthought. The bruising was extensive and a variety of black blue and yellow. Doctor. D. Was absolutely delighted with the outcome. Particularly the neck. That had, apparently, been something of a challenge, it had needed a lot of internal stitches and was very very changed. Despite her fragile state, Doctor. D. Was insistent that there should be daily facial massages to help the process of healing and to reduce the swelling. It seemed very brutal to push at the bruised skin around the neck and cheeks, Vicky wincing in pain as the fluid beneath was clearly moved about. Doctor. D. Swears by it, and his results speak for themselves so Vicky submitted to this twice daily torture. She was re-wrapped, her hair sticking out between the bandages like an unruly carrot top. She got to choose the colour of her outer bandages. It goes without saying, but I shall say it anyway, she chose pink.

It was a brutal way to see that new face. At least it was done. From now on, each fresh view would be showing improvement, we would never have to do that bit again. Vicky's lunch was a small pot of vanilla yoghurt, worked gradually into her barely open mouth with the baby spoon. It was an exhausting process for her, trying to get this little bit of nutrition in. I'm sure the effort involved far outweighed the calories ingested, but we had to try.

I felt like a swine, sitting next door eating real food, even the smell of it cooking seemed unnecessarily heartless. Vicky didn't complain though, and Lisa was determined I should look after myself too.

We needed more supplies, and Vicky couldn't be left so I decided to walk to the local supermarket with Lisa. I determined to make chicken casserole, mashed potatoes, stewed apples and custard. Comfort food, soft and mushy. Even if Vicky couldn't eat all of it, I could liquidize the mash with gravy from the casserole. I searched high and low for a potato masher but was more successful with a whisk for the custard. I'd only made custard from scratch once before, but I knew the general principal. What could possibly go wrong?

Walking back through the sunshine with my bag of winnings I felt all hunter gatherer. We are coping, I told myself. This is ok and I can deal with it. It was nice being out on my own, nobody knew me or anything about me. It was a kind of privacy.

The cooking gave me something positive and genuinely useful to do. So far I had only watched in awe as Lisa had expertly lubricated Vicky's eyes and helped her get the pills into her mouth. No mean feat, as Vicky's mouth was still almost entirely swollen shut. At least by cooking some familiar foods, I hoped I could bring a little bit of home, if only the smell, back to Vicky. Unfortunately right now, she couldn't smell anything. Her nose was still filled with wadding. When smell goes, as anyone who had had a blocked nose can testify, taste goes. Oh well, I thought, at least she can enjoy the texture.

Trying to cook chicken casserole on an electric ring hob intended for the reheating of pre-cooked waffles is a challenge. It was, with hindsight, probably rather over-ambitious and the mega mart could almost certainly have provided something I could have stuck in the microwave with almost identical outcome, but I was determined. This was the thing I could do to help and I was bloody well going to do it. I had to borrow a second saucepan from Angelique's room to make the mashed potatoes and my bain-marie for the custard was a danger to itself and others, being about as stable as a two-legged stool. Somehow, after an hour or so though, there was food. Vicky had a tiny cup of mash and gravy, and a baby spoon of custard before falling back exhausted on the pillow. It was a brave effort. I had considerably more of all of it and did indeed, feel comforted.

Angelique came to visit, she was going down to surgery the next morning. Knowing what we had just been through, understanding how she must be feeling I felt angry on her behalf. I didn't care how traumatized her family felt discovering their son, brother, whatever was female. No one should have to face such a procedure alone without a single good luck or get well soon. I was far less tolerant of other people's reactions than my own. Her family should, I felt, get over themselves and get with the programme. How quickly I had forgotten.

We fell into a pattern. It was hard to imagine we had ever done anything else. Lisa and I became a coordinated team, caring for Vicky day and night. Lisa took the night shift and I the day. Doctor. D. would visit every day, examining and changing the dressings. Vicky began to recover. The wadding came out of her nose, her eyes began to open more and the all covering bandages were replaced by what I can only call a 'face bra'. A combination of stretchy cotton and velcro strips, it was designed to reduce swelling and left Vicky's face encircled, like a nun awaiting the black cloth to go on top. Not a good look. The best thing though, was that I could finally see her eyes. 'There you are' I thought, 'I know you'. As Vicky recovered and began to look brighter, Lisa and I began to look more and more tired. It had been a tough few days, I admired Lisa hugely for all the care and skill she managed to deliver on so little sleep. We no longer had to carry Vicky to the bathroom, she could shuffle there herself. For longer trips, down to the restaurant on the ground floor, she had a wheelchair, but she was already trying to walk a little bit too. Her swelling was pretty bad, she looked not so much swollen as chubby. The tightness of her skin also made her look very young, more like a twenty something than someone in their early forties.

After a week Lisa was replaced by another carer, Jennifer. She was not as experienced as Lisa, but every bit as kind and Lisa was only ever a phone call away if Jennifer felt unsure about how to proceed. One last Doctor. D. Story. The day before I left Chicago, after he had examined Vicky for the umpteenth time, he turned to me and gave me the most backhanded compliment I have ever received. He stared at my face for a few moments and then said, 'I could make you beautiful'. The time was coming for me to go home.

I felt very strange about leaving Vicky in such a vulnerable state, but I wanted to see my children too and this was how we had planned it. I packed my bags and took a cab to the airport. On the plane the man sitting next to me got out his laptop and began reviewing his facial surgery patients photo by photo. Fine, I thought, whatever. I slept the whole way back.

These are the posts I made online from Chicago.

Hi ladies, I'm posting from Chicago in our hotel room, to let you all know that Vicky is, as we speak, in surgery having her facial feminisation surgery. She was already beautiful to me, but now maybe the whole world will get to see her true self. It's eight hours to go and counting so send all your prayers and thoughts and atheist positivity to Vicky and me.

I am happy to say we have met a lovely T-lady called Angie who is due for surgery on Thursday. She came and saw Vicky off to the clinic at 5 am and gave me a big hug, now we're going to go be shallow all day and look at clothes and shoes until it's time to go and pick my Vicky up and bring her back to the hotel to start recovery.

I bought Vicky a necklace just before we came here, it was rather expensive, but if she shouldn't have it then who?

It's a butterfly. Anyway, think of us and knowing Vicky as soon as she's conscious, she'll be posting!!!!

Tue Oct 26, 2010 6:42 pm
Quick update... Vicky is halfway through, the lower part of her face is done and now the brow and nose are being sorted. Thank you everyone for your kind thoughts and words. Like I say, if you catch Vicky posting in the next couple of days, smack her wrist and tell her to REST!!!

So here we are the day after surgery, about 12 hours since it finished. what a difference a day makes. Vicky is certainly uncomfortable, but she is able to sleep and eat and get to the loo and talk pretty clearly. The nurse, Lisa, is giving us wonderful support and being very gentle with Vicky as she administers the necessary medicines and cleaning schedules. Because of Vicky's underactive thyroid, the swelling may take a little longer than average to calm down, but, she's on her path and she never has to do yesterday again.

Thank you everyone for your words of support and encouragement. If you feel very brave go on Vicky's facebook page (Victoria Cantons), but probably not while you're eating...

Vicky is improving daily. Her dressings have been changed and so we had a chance to see (and photograph) her new face. If you're going down this road, I really recommend photographing such moments - not so you can do the world's most astonishing holiday snaps, but because it all happens pretty fast and though you get to look in the mirror you can't take it in fast enough before the dressings go back on.

After Doctor. D. came by yesterday (something akin to a small tornado passing through the hotel room!) Vicky and I were able to look quietly at the pictures in our own time and see the amazing changes that have happened.

On another note Liza, Vicky's nurse, and I have decided the appearance of the patient is in inverse proportion to the appearance of the care givers... in other words with each passing day Vicky looks better and better and Lisa and I look more and more zonked!

We're getting there

I think FFS is a bit like a rebirth you know, and at the moment Vicky is like a 4 month old, just starting on pureed food with a baby spoon... so no I'm afraid, no chocolate :-(but believe me as soon as she can manage it, she can have as much as she wants!

She is very swollen at the moment, but on a positive note, her mum called about an hour ago and said 'tell my daughter I love her'. Any of you who know Vicky's mother's previous level of acceptance will realize what a huge huge move forward that is.

Well, I'm off back to dear old Blighty! The cab comes to pick me up from the hotel in three hours and I have to leave Vicky behind to continue this journey on her own for the next week. Happily the wonderful Jennifer and Lisa, Doctor D.'s caregivers, are here to keep her safe and well. I spent the last two days on a cookathon making chicken casserole and bolognese sauce, mashed potatoes, cheese sauce and home made custard, (I really hope Jennifer can tell the difference between the last two, they look worryingly similar!)

Vicky is being incredibly brave about the three times a day face massage. It is brutal but necessary to remove the excess fluid from her swollen face poor love :-(Still, she knows it will be worth it. I've told her to send me pictures as she gradually improves because I want to understand every step of her journey.

I managed to upgrade to business class for the flight home which is a real blessing. I need to sleep and be ready when I get home because Rob is turning up with his support worker tomorrow evening and staying overnight... I really hope I stay awake.

Anyway, Vicky is doing wonderfully. I guess this is what the marriage vows meant - in sickness and in health. So, we are moving joyfully towards health.

Chapter Nine

B ack in London I had time to examine my own feelings over Vicky's facial surgery. They were complicated and Vicky didn't understand what it was that upset me. I tried to find other people who had been through the same experience, but as I've said before, the partners of transgendered women wouldn't fill a phone box.

I looked to the online support group, where Vicky was already posting regularly and excitedly about this latest part of her journey. I desperately wanted contact with any other women whose Trans partners had gone through facial feminization surgery. I understood that Vicky was simply revealing her true face, but it didn't seem unreasonable to be a bit sad, sometimes, for the face that had gone forever. I knew she was recovering from surgery and therefore not at her best, but when I admitted to her that I had shed some tears over the 'loss' of my male partner, she got upset with me, said I was 'false' and couldn't possibly celebrate her journey AND mourn the past at the same time. Of course I could. I knew this because it was exactly what I was doing but I felt pretty hurt to be told I wasn't being supportive enough. It was stupid really, obviously Vicky was not at her best and sitting in a hotel bed wrapped in bandages,surrounded by strangers and pumped full of pain killers. These statements represented her own anxieties rather than my behaviour, but even so, I felt let down. Vicky was still posting images of herself post-op on face book and now everyone could see, if they wanted, how completely unrecognizable she was from her old photos.

As soon as she was healed enough she planned to address her voice, next to facial surgery it sounded like a walk in the park. She hoped to be booked in for that procedure in the new year. It was a lot to put her body through, but with her new face her voice had become more inappropriate than ever. There was no question of asking Vicky to 'slow down' anymore, it was more a case of getting the rest of the surgery out of the way so we could get on with our lives again.

In a way the facial surgery did make it easier for me to let go of my husband. He was really gone now, my future was, very visibly, with Vicky. That isn't to say that I never felt a pang of regret or sadness. No matter how much I understood and accepted that truth, there still needed to be space for my grief.. I felt guilty letting Vicky see these moments, it felt disloyal, and I would try to hide them, but I think it would be naive to think she didn't know, or understand.

As I witnessed Vicky going through all this painful and invasive surgery, I wondered how much easier her life might have been had she been offered support before puberty kicked in and ravaged her body with testosterone. Wouldn't it be wonderful if children starting school were asked 'are you a boy or a girl?' Those who gave unexpected answers could be asked again at say 10. Sure some would reply ' good Lord did I say girl? how odd' (assuming a steady diet of P.G. Woodhouse over the last five years) but some, the transgendered ones, might say, 'yes, I feel like I got the wrong body' and then the appropriate counselling and support could be offered.

It's probably not as simple as that and maybe this is a completely mad idea, but watching Vicky, and many others, go through this grueling process in mid life made me think, surely surely there is a better way?

The next time I spoke to Vicky in Chicago she was celebrating. She had made it down to breakfast in the hotel , it was a first and a good step forward. Though the greasy sausage and egg were not what a woman needs when recovering from major facial surgery, the fact that she could put the fork in her mouth was progress. She continued to endure the massages of Doctor D. because she knew the outcome of all this would be as dependent on what was done now and in the next few months as what had been done in the eleven hours on Tuesday.

Sometimes I would get a bit tearful. A tiny bit of that was thinking about the face I would never see again, but only a tiny part. 95% was crying for the pain that Vicky had been enduring and continued to endure. Such a radical change of appearance was challenging for everyone around Vicky, but especially for her step kids and me. We had got used to so many things, we could get through this too. I hoped but I didn't know and the not knowing was frightening.

Ellie was anxious about seeing Vicky's new face for the first time. She was also angry. I kept telling her Vicky was concerned about how she would feel, but sometimes it didn't come out that way. She felt Vicky had taken this very drastic step too quickly. It was hard to explain why the surgery couldn't have waited. That difficulty was partly because I was not absolutely clear in my own head why it had all happened so fast. Fast is, of course, relative. For Vicky it was anything but fast. Forty years is a long time to wait just to see yourself in the mirror. It hadn't been forty years for me and the old fear still had power. If she really loved me, she would have waited, or more realistically, if she really loved me she would have been Anthony. I longed to be through all this. I longed for my heart to catch up with my brain, which perfectly well understood the realities of Vicky's situation. I didn't want to want Anthony anymore, because I definitely couldn't have him.

I still read a lot of posts on the online support forum from transgendered women who had lost both their relationship, and contact with their children, since transitioning. There was often a level of despair because they felt they were somehow unlikely and even unworthy to find love again. I wanted to say to them that Vicky and I had been through similar moments of despair. I had thought of leaving, I had declared that exposing the children to this 'female' was an impossibility. I wanted to let them see that it wasn't all over. That even these things could change, with time. Love was still out there.

The second week was over and Vicky was coming home. I was relieved and looking forward to having her safely back in the UK, but I was worried. I didn't know how Vicky would look when she got off the plane. She had had another week of healing since I had seen her. From the phone calls we had had, it was obvious that she was able to talk more freely and was much more mobile, I was even worried that I wouldn't recognize her, which was ridiculous. To my shame, I was still to embarrassed to kiss her full on the lips in the middle of Heathrow airport, but I did hug her. I wish I wasn't so afraid of how other people would react to two women kissing, or to a woman and a transgendered woman, or to, well anyway, I wish I wasn't such a coward.

Vicky had to wear the 'face bra' all the time for the first four months, which did something to hide the full extent of stitches and scarring from Ellie. Even so it was quite a shocking thing to be confronted with, and she was pretty good about it. She even managed to give Vicky a gentle hug. There is certainly no better way to dissuade your teen from plastic surgery. The cold hard realities of a face cut, swollen and bruised, the joins looking more like poorly stitched blankets than invisible scars, would surely be enough to put off all but the most determined. I don't really consider Vicky's facial surgery as cosmetic. That suggests a level of choice that wasn't there. Had she not had the surgery there is no question that many more people would still be treating her as male and responding poorly to the fact she was in a dress. That kind of thing can wear you down, day after day.

Whatever the rights and wrongs of it, the surgery was a done deal. It would improve of course but none of us would forget that initial sight. Another hurdle overcome, we got on with life.

A few days later, came a moment I had not been looking forward to. Vicky's scalp had been seriously remodeled and held together with, I kid you not, staples. These staples now had to be removed. The device for achieving this was almost identical to the one for removing staples from paper. A small metallic jaw with two sharp teeth at either corner, top and bottom. Doctor D. Had blithely suggested that this was an ideal job for me. He's a surgeon, I expect he's used to hoiking metal out of people's flesh. I was less blasé. The staples ran from behind the bottom of Vicky's ears up into her hairline. There were dozens of them. It was vile and exactly as you might imagine it so I won't describe it anymore than to say there was a noise as you pulled the staple out and a level of tug required and, well yes, that's quite enough of that.

That fun little task behind us, it only remained to keep Vicky in hand-washed face-bras and regularly and liberally apply moisturiser to her eyes. She now had to continue the facial massage herself. It had been suggested I might help with this, and I tried it once, but really it was more than I could do to inflict such direct pain on her so I'm afraid I left her to manage on her own.

It was behind us. I knew there was still the small matter of genital surgery to come but really compared to what had just been done I found it hard to believe it could be any worse. Vicky had at one point been considering surgery on her two middle toes, which were a triumph of individuality against evolution, they were better designed to cling to a branch than fit into shoes. It meant she could only wear size elevens. If they were shortened she might get into size nines, which would open up a world of possibility to her inner Imelda Marcos. Now though still bruised and swollen from facial surgery, with the prospect of imminent vocal and eventual genital surgery, signing up for yet another operation didn't seem that tempting. I understand some people get almost addicted to the wonders of plastic surgery, unable to stop tinkering with their own appearance. Vicky was not going to be one of those. Enough was enough.

Family and friends were astonished at what had been achieved, more than one of them now said they could see the reality of the woman that Vicky had always claimed to be. It had worked. We got stared at in the street because a face-bra is an attention grabbing object, but the point is people would say, 'what happened to her'. No-one saw a man anymore. They saw a woman who had undergone facial surgery. Often newer friends would question if she had needed anything doing at all. They had no idea how much she had had done. It was all very gratifying. Of course once Vicky opened her mouth they would look again. It was the biggest remaining problem. Her voice.

Vicky had been attending speech therapy for some time now, both in groups and one to one. She tried so hard to modulate her voice, but it had always been a very deep rich manly voice and it was not responding to exercise and thinking differently. Vicky found it very frustrating, and so, I have to admit did I. The moment she spoke, shop assistants, waiters, anyone on a phone, assumed she was male. Even if she corrected them and said, 'It's madam actually', they would more often then not reply, 'sorry about that, now what can I help you with sir?'.

To add to the problem, Vicky herself found it very hard to hear how she sounded to other people. In her head she would hear a warm female voice and then be upset at yet again being called 'sir'. When she did find a pitch that everyone around her, including me, accepted as sounding female, she felt false, as though she were putting on a comedy mouse voice. Surely that couldn't be what she must sound like for the rest of her life? Vicky's vocal problems were so much more complicated than the thickness or tension of her vocal chords. They were wrapped up in a lifetime of hiding her true self away, trying desperately to embrace the man she wasn't. Now after forty years of hiding, her voice wasn't there, or if it was, she was too afraid to use it.

The speech therapist agreed that therapy alone could only achieve so much, but she was also very clear that surgery was not a magic fix. Before and after surgery Vicky would have to practice regularly, focus on every word she uttered. As a thoughtful and considered speaker, Vicky already seemed to focus on the meaning of every word she uttered and this could make her appear hesitant at times, or worse, as though she hadn't heard the question (It's in our top ten things we quarrel about list, right next to Vicky's inability to use an indicator when driving and my inability to put the lid back on anything..ever). The thought of adding another layer of hesitancy worried me.

Part of me, as with the facial surgery, wanted to tell her that how other people perceived her, or us, was their problem. She was transgendered, she would have a deep voice, so what. Vicky of course was never going to go for that. Though she supported anyone's choice not to have surgery and to present to the world as a woman with male attributes, she didn't want to be one of them. She just wanted to be like any other woman. It's all very well singing 'I am what I am', but if no one understands what you are it's hard to stay confident.

In July 2010 Vicky finally had the vocal surgery. She was in and out in one day, but not allowed to speak, or so much as whisper for three days. Instead she had a notebook and paper. This worked perfectly well if you were standing next to her and could be alerted to the communication by a prod in the ribs, but as she was resting in bed and I was getting on with life downstairs, it was very frustrating. Vicky also discovered the frustrations not just of not being able to communicate the big things - The house is on fire, Your daughter has eloped with our neighbour, that kind of thing - she also missed the minutiae of conversation. One afternoon as we were out doing the weekly shop, she pulled me over and began frantically writing in her notepad. I put down the bags I'd been lugging to the car and waited in silence as Vicky scribbled away.

Finally she passed me the paper and I read the urgent message, 'Isn't that a new Paperchase'. Worth waiting for I think you'll agree. Well, it was only for three days and yes, it was very quiet.

Vicky had to be examined by the doctor again to make sure she was ready to speak. When the moment came her voice was very quiet. Not squeaky, but not as dark and rich as before either. It was a partial success. The bottom third, the chest voice had definitely been erased, but Vicky continued to find it hard to raise her voice higher than it's middle range. There's no question that she was disappointed. No matter how much you are told that an operation is not a magic fix-all, part of you must still secretly hope that you'll wake up sounding like Marilyn Monroe. I was, if I'm honest, a little relieved. Not because I'd been secretly hoping the pitch wouldn't shift, I wanted the operation to succeed as much as Vicky did, but the truth is I could still recognize the voice, like her face it was changed but still related. Anthony's sister's voice.

In speech therapy sessions she could read passages and passages in a light piping tone, which sounded utterly feminine, but she just could not do it outside of the session. Our counsellor pointed out that she had become reliant on her speech therapy sessions as the place where her voice would work. The reality was if she could do it in the safety of speech therapy, she could do it anywhere. There was no mechanical reason why she couldn't talk like that all the time.

Vicky struggled with this for a long time. One day quite recently she was speaking to an old friend on the phone and he suddenly said 'that's too feminine'. No, I thought, that's how she's meant to sound. It comes and goes, but considering all the changes Vicky has managed to make, I think she'll get there when she's ready. Just don't ask her to sing.

As Christmas 2010 approached my annual obsession with how many cards we sent and how many we got reared its ugly head. I don't know why I focused on this so much. Writing about it now I want to give myself a firm slap, or at least a gentle shake, but the truth is at the time it mattered to me. I tried, while posting online, to talk myself out of this petty example of self pity, but I seem to remember it didn't work.

> *In years gone by we have sent and received around 100 christmas cards, we're friendly folk and I do love christmas. This year, I'm sad to say, looks like being a repeat of last year, we're down to about ten. Since Vicky's transition, maybe I should say 'our' transition, because we have certainly been through this together, we have lost many many acquaintances and not a few friends. The Christmas card tally is a rather visible record of this and it's a bit depressing. Yet I know we are lucky. Our families are still speaking to us, we do have good friends who have stuck by us, we are not isolated or ostracized. I wish it were so for all transgendered people, but I know it isn't. So this is a virtual Christmas card to everyone who is alone this Christmas simply for being honest about who they are. I think you're all amazing and the world is a better place for having you in it. Happy Christmas x*

That last bit is something I believe deeply. The world is a better place for being diverse. There is a running debate about whether society should seek to eliminate disability, not by improving the individuals capacities, but by stopping them being born in the first place. Think, the argument goes, of all the suffering, not to mention expense, that could be avoided if disabled people were never born. Genetic testing holds the power to predict more and more of the conditions that affect people's lives. We could, theoretically, eliminate them. I assume that argument would extend to intersex people. The argument against such a plan beside the religious one that, 'all life is sacred', says, ' Look what we would lose. Look at

Einstein, what about Stephen Hawking?' The truth to me though, is that these differences are not only precious when they are counterbalanced by some extraordinary talent or genius. My life has been immeasurably enriched by having my son. The world is a better, more interesting place for having him in it. My life has been immeasurably enriched by having Vicky in it. I'm only going to live this life once and my experience now contains the astonishing truth of Vicky's life, of watching a woman emerge from the cocoon of an apparent man. It's all worth having and celebrating. Still. I would have liked more Christmas cards.

Christmas 2010, with all the family, came and went. It was a much happier time than the previous year. It felt like we had all come a very long way. Things that at the time had seemed insurmountable were now only memories we didn't bother revisiting. All the resentment I had felt towards my family ebbed away. I was now able to step back and understand with much more balance. They had, each one of them, only been making their journeys. That was all. My anger, no, my fear had come from that same old familiar place. To my mother and my sister all I was really saying was, 'if you really loved me...', and all they were doing was saying it right back at me. We all of us feared that each other's reactions signaled a diminution of the love we felt for each other, and of course we were wrong. How useful it would have been to understand that in the first place. It would have made the whole thing easier if we could have known there would come a time when we were all together as a family and the fact that part of that family was Vicky was neither here nor there.

By January, Vicky no longer needed to wear the hideous face-bra. Her stitches had mostly dissolved and the swelling was going down noticeably. No one stared at us any more. I'm sure our local community was well used to seeing us out and about, but even so, and this may have been entirely in my head, it felt like we were blending in more. I wasn't afraid to walk down the road with her anymore. The thought of going to the cinema filled me only with pleasure and not the anxiety of potential reactions. What a shame we couldn't have had all this without eleven hours of surgery. Still, we did have it and it was good.

Every now and then a hornet would escape from the bottom of Vicky's emotional Pandora's box. She could still become very angry or very tearful. It was not easy especially as my capacity for 'yes dear' was not strong and all too easily things would explode, but we talked it through. We always talked it through in the end. We'd got very good at talking things through. We had continued the weekly counselling sessions up in central London and they had become, not a crutch exactly, but a time to look forward to when both of us knew we could raise and discuss the things that were hurting us and then be rid of them. Afterwards there was lunch and strolling around shops and maybe going to the cinema. It was a nice day out combined with the emotional equivalent of a deep facial cleanse.

It seems strange to say that the main part of Vicky's transition was behind us, when her gender reassignment surgery was yet to come - but in terms of our daily lives, that was just packaging. I'm not saying Vicky wasn't still desperate to get it done and frustrated by the slowness of the progress within the NHS. but the truth was the woman was already here, not waiting to be created by a bit of flesh being repositioned. We could, to a very large degree, just get on with life, thank God. Some people loved us, some didn't, the same as everyone else. It was normality and we were ok.

Life was normal, and that included death. On February the 11th 2011, my dad died. He had been in the wonderful theatrical nursing home, Denville Hall for a decade and a half. He had lived his last years in dignity and comfort. The staff were tireless and wonderful. It had all been as good as it could have been, which was pretty awful really. In the last few years his speech had all but disappeared, reduced to the concise pairing of 'Love' and 'Fuck off', (said with all the humour a man of three words could muster).

His head had gradually fallen to one side, which made eating and drinking really hard and he was in a wheelchair, reduced to one working limb, his left arm. Though we'd set him up with a piano in his room, he only played it twice to my knowledge. In the last months of his life I took to playing for him all the songs he had taught me as a child. Gershwin's best, 'Summertime', 'S'wonderful', 'Our love is Here to Stay'. The lyrics said all the things he couldn't.

I didn't ever tell him about Vicky. He had been so happy to know I was loved and cared for, and I still was, so why complicate things. He had blotted his son's death from his consciousness. If we ever mentioned Matthew, or even Matthew's sons, Dad would look away, whistle, laugh or sing. He was having none of it. His mind was balanced between the control of his epilepsy and the control of his madness. A bearable medium had been achieved, not too many fits, calmly bonkers. It seemed unnecessarily indulgent to insist he process the complexities of a transgendered daughter-in-law. The impact of that was that Vicky didn't come with me to see him until he was nearing the end, and then she waited outside in the car. I hope she didn't feel I was ashamed of her, because I wasn't, but I can see it may not have seemed that way.

Two years before he had come close to dying, going into a series of seizures every thirty seconds or so for a couple of days. It was awful and none of us wanted him to have to go like that. In the end he didn't. The nurse who sat with him as we all tried and failed to get there in time to say one last goodbye, held his hand as he breathed gently out. He didn't breathe in again. That was it. He went gently into that good night full of love for all of us and knowing we loved him. S'wonderful.

Vicky was invited, but couldn't come, to the funeral, which was a great shame. I had imagined this would be the moment I would introduce her to the staff at Denville Hall, show them who had been my back-up all this time It just wasn't possible, but then my sister's husband couldn't be there either so we were all in the same boat. I wanted Vicky there also to meet my extended family, many of whom had only heard about her transformation had been ready to welcome her, as herself. It felt like an opportunity missed, but it did at least show me that everyone knew about Vicky and me, and no one minded a bit.

A death is a good reminder of what is important in life. Dad had not been the best fun for a lot of his life with us. We experienced fear and anger, resentment and indifference. Somehow, we had all ended up at Love. It reminded me, as if I needed reminding, that Love, still, and always, is the answer.

Two months after dad's funeral I went into a recording studio and made an album of all those wonderful Gershwin songs. I had played in local pubs with a trio for a couple of years before this all happened, but I hadn't sung since Vicky told me she was transgendered. The emotional honesty required had shut down in me. I had become a carrier of unspeakable secrets, and then, once it was no longer a secret, I had been so confused about what I felt that the last thing I could do was sing about it. Now I could sing again, and not only that, I could sing about 'he' and not burst into tears. It was just a song. Vicky had felt very frustrated that I had stopped singing and had been pressing me for some time to do a pub gig or at least get together with my band and have a play. She felt my inability to do so indicated a deep lack of acceptance and made all my words hollow.

I wanted her to accept me even if I never sang another note, and to try and understand why I might find it difficult to sing ' The Man I Love' . All I can say is that it took the time it took. It was a grieving process. Now though, it was fun again and I didn't need to cry. I had love and I could sing about it. Several of the tracks were a tone lower than I used to sing them, and my mother, fine musician that she is, noticed. She asked if this voice drop was because I was 'now a lesbian'. I think she was joking. Probably.

Chapter Ten

I'm not really bothered if people label me as lesbian, bi, or whatever. It's 'single' that annoys me. It's the dismissal of my relationship with Vicky and the assumption that I am available that insults the truth of what I have with Vicky. Love. The real deal, fought for and won through despite some pretty difficult circumstances. I don't regard myself as having married a man who decided to be a woman instead. I married a person whom I believed to be male who turned out to be a transgendered woman. She was born that way, and that, at some level, is who I fell in love with. Unless I need T-shirts printed in the future, I don't need any other word for that relationship than 'real'.

Vicky and I have different experiences of the reactions to us as a couple. She sometimes finds people expressing surprise that she has a partner. Surely as a Transgendered woman she is not only abandoned and despised but obviously undesirable, seems to be the general wisdom. To me, however, the reaction has an annoying extra. Men, more often than not, seem to read, ' in a relationship with a transgendered woman' as 'not in a real relationship at all and just waiting for a proper man'. This is expressed not only in a level of flirting that I didn't experience when I was perceived to be married to a man, but in direct questions about what I 'surely must be missing'.

It seems to me that such reading of me as single and available is another form of transphobia. I'm not looking for sympathy here, believe me I can handle stupid comments, but I'm getting a bit tired of it. Our friends are friendly and accepting of us as a couple (the ones that weren't are no longer our friends) but others continue to make this dismissive assumption. This strange underlying attitude feels insulting. Vicky is reasonable for wanting to be with me because I'm 'normal', but I, a 'normal' person, am unreasonable to wish to be with her. Unable to believe it might be love, attraction etc. etc. It is decided my motivation must be failure to find anything better or worse still, not wanting to lose the pretty house and garden. All I'm saying is, It ain't necessarily so. Apart from all of which, I resent the idea that I'm 'normal'. Who wants to be THAT.

The truth is, we are living a life that seemed impossible two years ago. I wanted to share this experience because transition can be hell, for the person themselves, and for their loved ones around them. Writing this has helped me understand what happened more clearly. We went to hell. It wasn't very nice, but I think we had to go, when you're blowing up mountains nothing less will do, and it was worth it.

This is the place we didn't believe we could get to. It seemed impossible even to visualize the outcome that would work and make everyone happy. We had lived for six years together as a man and a woman. I had been happy, Vicky had been miserable. At first it seemed as though we had just swapped roles. Vicky would be happy and I would be miserable. Neither situation would do, but how to get over the rainbow? Over the rainbow is like this. Vicky is Vicky.. all the time and I am me. Everyone we know, knows we are more in love than ever and happy and relaxed as a same-sex couple. That required quite a major shift of understanding from me about myself. It took me a while to understand that Vicky was not the only one transitioning. Then it took me a while to get over the fact that I hadn't had a choice in 'outing' myself as being in a same-sex relationship. Some people respond to that by saying, 'Oh, has she had THE operation then. The answer to that comes in two parts. Part one: None of your business. Part two: That's not what made Vicky a woman. (Part three: see part one).

Our children are happy, this didn't destroy their lives. Ellie, now 18 is at art college. All her friends have met Vicky, no bricks have been thrown, our windows remain intact. My son, now 22 is at mainstream music college studying rock guitar, he loves to talk rock music with Vicky and we visit every couple of weeks. Of the two of them I would say my boy generally wears more make-up. No one stares. We are living our lives. We take Ellie out to lunch and do the shopping, we feed the cat and watch Strictly Come Dancing. We are normal as the next family.

It wasn't always like this but now it is. Life, is not a photograph, it's a film. In fact, it's not a film, it's life. Many of the friendships I thought were lost forever, gradually recovered. They are not quite the same as they were before, but the really heartening thing is that people have continued to try. To understand that this is not a lifestyle choice for Vicky, but a physical abnormality that had to be put right, a medical condition that was resolved. I am very touched that my friends felt the friendship we had before was worth saving. Where before some saw only the selfishness of a person for whom self-expression, at any cost, was all, they now see courage. I think too that my friends struggled to understand why I was staying. Someone once said to me, 'but you're not a lesbian'. Well, I'm sleeping with a transgendered woman so that depends on what you mean by lesbian. Some feminists see transgendered women as wolves in sheep's clothing, men who have engaged in an elaborate subterfuge to steal even the physical form from 'real' women creating a parody of womanhood based on male perceptions. They would not describe me as a lesbian. Some lesbians reportedly regard transgendered women as men who are trying to trick them into having sex with a man, much as some men fear they will be 'tricked' into having sex with a man who 'looks' like a woman. I genuinely believe that is a misunderstanding of what a transgendered woman is. For those though who do accept Vicky as female, then yes, I'm a lesbian. As far as Vicky and I are concerned we're both spoken for, so it doesn't really enter into it.

I was told, often, that others didn't think they would have stayed had they found themselves in my position. All I can say to that is,

I don't think you can know what you would do until you're here. It certainly wasn't my plan 'A'. For the first year at least I don't think I knew what I was doing or what I was going to do. My planning shrank to a simple, 'what's next'. Sometimes I longed to be able to walk away, to imagine a life uncomplicated by transgender issues. I didn't stay because I couldn't leave. I stayed because I wanted to, because being with Vicky makes me happy and being without her makes me miserable. It's all very selfish really. My understanding, even Vicky's understanding of herself, has evolved through this process. The simple truth is, we want to be together.

I still miss Anthony, but I understand what happened to him, she survived. I survived too, and was changed by this experience. It took me, as the phrase goes, out of my comfort zone and freed me from my need for privacy, well diminished my need for privacy anyway. I am a much happier person for that. It forced me to examine who I was and what I believed. Not what I said I believed, but what I was actually willing to fight for. I regret some of my behavior. I wish I had had more wisdom and more courage, that I had been kinder and more understanding of challenges other than my own. I particularly wish that I'd understood other people's feelings more quickly, but then I wish I had long blonde hair and fit size 10 jeans. Better to take on life as yourself than as who you wish you were I suppose.

I hope it has also shown my children that they are lovely and acceptable as themselves. Whatever they do with their lives, whoever they turn out to be, they are perfect in my eyes and always will be. Even if they end up heterosexual solicitors, married with two children and a golden retriever, I shall always love them for being them. Shakespeare was right (huge surprise) 'to thine own self be true'. Sometimes easier said than done, but worth the effort.

We have not lost our family's support, our mothers still love us and the house is full at Christmas. I've stopped counting the cards. We have many lovely friends. We know how lucky we are.

On the twelfth of May, 2012, Victoria and I renewed our marriage vows. We hired a venue, a band and a pyramid of cupcakes with butterflies on them. We both wore spectacular dresses and tiaras. We had ninety guests and sat down to roast lamb and monkfish. We kept telling everyone it wasn't a wedding, we already had one of those thank you. The truth is though it absolutely was a wedding, because this is when I stood before all my family and friends and said, 'Victoria, I choose you' and this is when Victoria stood in front of all her family and friends and said 'I, Victoria, choose you Emma'. The fact that this was a wedding only dawned on Vicky and me when we entered the ballroom in Putney and were hit by a wall of love. Everyone cheering and clapping and celebrating our love for each other, we were completely astounded and moved. Our dear friend Caroline Grayson, an interfaith minister, guided us through the words we had chosen to say to each other.

I went first. "Three years ago I thought I had lost you. I did not understand what was happening. I didn't know where our future was or how it could be. I thought I would lose my friends, my family, everyone. But I did not lose you. I found you, and in finding you, I found myself. I did not lose my family, or my friends. We all fought through and we won. The promises I made to you seven years ago were promises. Today they are our truths. I will always love you and I will always be there for you, in sickness and in health, for better for worse, til death sends us on the next part of our journey. I am yours"

Vicky said, "Dear Emma, I stand before you in astonishment and wonder at the commitment you have given to our marriage and relationship. I pledge to love you, to cherish you, to trust you and to face all of life together with you. I vow to be loyal to you that all my memories and imagination will be shared with you. Through all the sacrifices, joy, the laughter and the tears. All I am, all I have, all I will be and all I can be I pledge to you. To love and support you, to care for you until my dying breath. Lastly, in the words from our wedding day in 2005:

> Like Screws unravelling
> From their bolts
> Like a book trying to stand with a broken spine.
> Like a cloud dissolving as
> The rain pours down
> Like a door unhinging
> It's bolts undone
> I am nothing without you,
> Like DNA, it's matrix unspiraling
> I am nothing without you

Emma, thank you for standing next to me as I vow to stand next to you."

I blubbed, Victoria blubbed, Caroline blubbed. Everyone joined in. When we'd finished our vows we danced to Nat King Cole's 'Let there be love'

and we knew it was the answer.

Epilogue

I wonder what Vicky and I will be like in thirty years time. There doesn't appear to be any research on the effect of a transgendered woman taking female hormones for thirty of forty years, but it may not be entirely safe, long-term. It may, as any HRT can, increase the risks of high blood pressure, strokes, heart disease, even some kinds of cancer. There may be side effects that don't happen to non-transgendered women, that may happen to Vicky, but then I may die in a freak chocolate fudge factory accident long before that. I hope we get there. A pair of old dears holding hands on the bus, making jam for the church fete and being spoken to politely in case we're shocked. I don't imagine at that stage anyone will have the slightest idea that one of us used to look like a man. I don't imagine we'll ever talk about it. I think we've talked about it enough to last us a lifetime.

When I married Anthony, I thought I had found the fairytale. The tall dark handsome man who I loved and who loved me. He was everything I wanted, but he couldn't stay, because, some of him wasn't real. It turned out it wasn't the most important part, but it still hurt to lose it. What I really needed was a new fairytale. So here it is:

Once upon a time there was a beautiful princess. She had been locked in a tower since she was a baby and nobody knew she was there. Everybody thought it was just a tower. It was a very useful tower and people came to live in its shade, they built their houses and planted their fields. Everyone was very happy. Except the princess of course. She was trapped. She shouted out to the villagers, "Help, I'm trapped in here, I'm a princess!", but no one listened.

One day the princess decided to knock down the tower brick by brick. As she started throwing the bricks down to the ground the villagers shouted, "Hey stop that, that's our tower" but she wanted to be free so she kept throwing bricks down. Some landed on the fields and one went straight through the roof of a house and broke a chair. Everyone was very angry. When the whole tower was just a pile of rubble the princess stepped out into the fresh air. She was covered in dust and no one believed she was a princess, she looked more like a bit of the tower. One of the villagers walked up to her and asked "Why did you ruin our tower?"

"I was trapped" said the princess "But no one knew I was there."

Most of the villagers didn't really believe her and they laughed at her, but one villager, called Emma, who was exceptionally gorgeous and wise and had a picnic basket of destiny said, "You are very brave and beautiful. You better come and live with me. Even though the tower was a useful part of the village, I didn't know anyone was trapped in it and we'd much rather have you than a tower that was really a prison."

And they all lived happily ever after. (despite Emma never putting the lids back on anything... ever.)

The End

Also Available

From Andrews UK

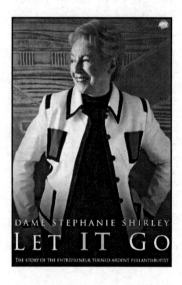

Let IT Go

Dame Stephanie Shirley

Dame Stephanie Shirley is one of Britain's leading philanthropists and has donated most of her life to helping good causes, especially those close to her heart. This fascinating memoir charts Dame Stephanie's life from her time as a child in Germany and arrival in England as an unaccompanied Kindertransport refugee through to her retirement and dedication to charity. It is an amazing read which will take you through the entire range of emotions - from happiness at the success of her original company Freelance Programmers through to the ultimate sadness of losing her only child.